FIVE FLIGHTS UP

FIVE FLIGHTS UP

Sex, Love, and Family, from Paris to Lyon

Kristin Louise Duncombe

This work is a memoir based on my life in France, and the details within are true insofar as memory serves. However, the names and identifying characteristics of some of the people in my story have been shuffled and disguised, so as to protect their privacy. Those who have been named gave their consent.

1 Expat Families 2 Trailing Spouses 3 Marriage 4 France 5 Personal Identity

For my family

PARIS 2009

One

How can you be sick of living in *Paris?* This is my incredulous comment when Tano claims that after eight years, he's had enough. Enough of the big city life. Enough of the cost of living. Enough of our family of four crammed into a 635-square-feet apartment. We are sitting in a little café off the place des Vosges. With its elegant covered archways, warm cafés, and trendy art galleries giving out to a tree-lined square, this is one of my very favorite places in Paris. But what I thought was going to be a special after work drink with my husband—a rare indulgence given our family schedule—has instead revealed itself as the chosen stage for his announcement: He has received a job offer, out of the blue, an offer that would force us to change our lives by moving to Lyon, a smaller city in eastern-central France, 293 miles from Paris in the region called the Rhône-Alpes.

"Let's do it," he says, waving for the waiter, who has studiously ignored us for the last ten minutes. "Let's try something new."

"But I have zero desire to move," I say, amazed that he could think that I would ever tire of Paris. Aside from being one of the most beautiful places on this planet, the city had provided the answer to my long-standing need to create a fixed home somewhere in the world.

Until Paris, moving dominated my existence. I lived all over the world, changing countries every couple of years as a child and teenager—from the United States to the Ivory Coast to Egypt to India to Indonesia—because of my father's career with the US Foreign Service. Shortly after returning to the United States as a young adult, I met Tano, a sexy Argentinean doctor, and after a whirlwind romance, followed him to East Africa—first Kenya, then Uganda—where he worked as a doctor with Médecins Sans Frontières.

"First of all," Tano continues, as though he hasn't even heard me, "The cost of living in Lyon is much better than Paris..."

His voice fades to a distant hum as I recall how the East-African chapter of our life led to an infidelity that almost destroyed our marriage. I fled to Paris with our toddler, Carmen, where we owned a tiny apartment that we had as yet never lived in.

"...And imagine living in a place where people are not so, so...*hostile.*" He reaches out and taps the back of the waiter, now clearing an abandoned table. "Is it too much to ask you for two glasses of red, please? This is a restaurant, no?"

Parisians can be, shall we say, *difficult,* it's true, but I am in love with this place, and that alone allows me to forgive its flaws.

And Tano should too, as it was my new life in Paris that ultimately fashioned our reconciliation. After a separation that dragged out over months, Carmen took her father back immediately, with the easy unconditionality of a child. At not even three years old, she had no notion of our falling out, much less the difficulty of forgiving and forgetting.

But it was not as easy for me, plagued as I was by the need, fueled by jealousy and hurt, to re-examine every aspect of our life together, not least of which the question: How had I, an ambitious young career woman, ended up totally dependent on a man—and on top of it, one who betrayed me?

When we split up, I had no job. No income. Nothing of my own, save for the small apartment in Paris that Tano and I had invested every last dime in, in the hopes that we would move there one day.

I could have gone running back to the States, to the open arms of my parents and two sisters—not that there was even enough money left over to buy plane tickets. Of course my father made it patently clear that all I had to do was say the word and he would see to it that Carmen and I were on the next plane to Washington, DC.

The fact that I was thirty-two years old, however, when this personal catastrophe struck made running back to my parents' home feel impossible, like a regression to being a dependent child. The need to stand on my own two feet and be a self-reliant *adult* was pressing, a developmental task that I had to complete.

But oh, dear Reader, let me tell you how awful it was to be in this situation: totally broke and financially dependent on the husband I just left. With all of our savings invested in the apartment, our only income was Tano's small paychecks. It was a bleak and formative moment in my life, being confronted with what it really meant to not have a way to support my child and myself.

But I did have the 635 square feet on rue Oberkampf.

And so, to Paris I went, for the first time in my life making a geographic move that I settled on entirely by myself. Until that very moment my path around the world had no logical connection other than the professional obligations of the two most important men in my life: my father and my husband.

With hindsight, this was an electrifying, exhilarating moment in my personal development. I didn't realize it then, but looking back I see that more than a departure from my unhappy marriage and move from Africa to Europe, the major journey I embarked on was an identity shift: from one who follows to one who leads.

"So you see," Tano says, his conviction breaking into my reverie. "In Lyon we'll be able to live in a much bigger space. Even food and transport are cheaper."

Food? Transport? He acts like we're planning a vacation. This is my *life* we're talking about, and it's a life I am deeply attached to. Eight years in—longer than I have ever lived anywhere—I have been able to build the things that I now feel an almost murderous sense of protectiveness over: a stable home for our family (that has expanded to include a son, Lorenzo, six years Carmen's junior), a wonderful network of friends, a fantastic professional life.

Eight years after my tremulous arrival in Paris, I am at the height of my career. I am on contract with the American University of Paris to provide counseling services to their students. I frequently speak in the international school and Embassy circuits about raising "global and mobile" kids, a term I branded to describe the international children I see in my practice, mother in my home, and was myself while growing up. Most significant is my work with trailing spouses, helping them to navigate the identity loss, depression, and anxiety that can erupt by having to move around the world because of someone else's obligations.

The waiter sets two glasses of wine on our table, with what appears to be a conciliatory smile. Tano and I clink our glasses and the waiter says, "*santé*"—to health. We sip our wine quietly, lost in our own thoughts, as the sound of a melancholy aria drifts from some distant corner of the plaza, accompanied by the soft strains of a violin. I have heard this musical duo so many times over these years in Paris, and still, those first notes never cease to move me, as though I am discovering something beautiful for the first time.

"So what about it? What about leaving the big city for Lyon?"

"But what about *my* life?"

"You can start over," Tano says.

"It's not so easy to just 'start over' when you're in business for yourself."

"True, but *you're* good at it," Tano says.

The capacity for reinvention is a hallmark of people who have moved a lot, so I do know that I can start over in Lyon, if I just work hard enough. But the professional scene will never be able to match that of Paris, where there is an enormous community of expats seeking therapy services, and where an American University will hire me to run their counseling program.

"Let me remind you," he continues, "Lyon is also an international city. There's the World Health Organization, Interpol's headquarters, all the big pharmaceuticals…"

From there he starts in on the great pleasures of living in a city that has two rivers running through it—the Rhône and the Saône. When he raves about the Alps being visible from the city center on a clear day, I'm already in a miserable meditation around dismantling my private practice.

"And if you can't find enough work to go full time, you can do something else," Tano cajoles, "like write another book."

This snaps me back to attention. The first and only book I have ever written—*Trailing: A Memoir*—deals with the exact topic we are haggling over right now: *me* following *him* around the world.

"Oh my God," I gape. "You must *really* want me to move."

He snorts, a sort of half laugh, and I know that he is remembering his reaction to me writing about our marriage. In fact, when he finished reading the first draft of *Trailing*, he took a pen and replaced the title with *My Husband is a Jerk*.

"How can you write all those horrible things about me?" he had demanded.

"The character in the book is frustrated and angry, Tano."

"The 'character' in the book is you, *Querida*, and you're talking about *me*."

I re-worked the text, and re-worked it some more, until the story moved away from the critical, blaming stance it had once stood on and focused more squarely on my needy impracticality at the time we lived in East Africa, and the major lesson borne of our marital crisis: That Tano and I needed to have equal shots at pursuing our dreams—professional and personal—if our marriage was going to survive. After everything we'd been through, becoming financially self-sufficient went hand in hand with this for me, and it was only after I was settled in Paris and earning a proper living that I could gauge I was still in the marriage because I *wanted* to stay. Staying when *I didn't have to because I was able to support myself* was all the proof I needed that our relationship had truly healed.

But does one ever fully recover from a spouse's affair?

That question comes roaring back as Tano's insistence that I follow him to Lyon causes me to seize up in panic. Leaving my hard-earned professional existence will mean that my earnings will plummet to zero; I will relinquish all of my financial power. I know it isn't fair to obsess about this now—our marriage has been on the right track for years, and Tano has made more than a heartfelt case for his good intentions. But the body seems to have a mind of its own, because no matter what I know rationally, giving up my professional and financial stability fills me with fear.

Give up *my* life for *ours*?

Give up my life for his?

Two

The argument about moving to Lyon continues for several weeks, but I do not waver: *I'm not moving.*

"But *Kreestin*," Tano pleads one morning as we gulp our coffee. "I have to give an answer about the job."

"Just *take* it," I say, exasperated that he is bugging me about this as I am trying to get the family out the door for the day. Carmen is hollering from the other room that she can't find her shoes, Lorenzo is still in his PJs, and I don't have time to bicker about this *again* this morning.

"*Take* the job?" Tano says, following on my heels as I search for Carmen's shoes. "Does that mean you'll move?"

"No!" I snap, as I find them behind the curtains. "Get dressed, Lorenzo!" I shout as I drop the shoes in front of Carmen and pluck a wet towel off the floor. I hang it on a doorknob and face Tano. "*You* go."

"Without you?"

"We'll have a commuter relationship. Lots of people do that."

"That is not a normal way to live."

But to me it feels entirely normal. Ever since we have been married Tano has been constantly coming and going. It feels abnormal to be together all the time. Those rare periods when he is suddenly home with say, two months without travel, we get irritable with each other. I remind him of this.

"That's because we live in 635 tiny square feet. The whole point of moving is so that we can have a *normal* life."

My skin prickles every time Tano complains that our life on rue Oberkampf is not "normal." We live on the third floor of a six-story building, inhabited by families that have melded into such a close-knit community that I christened it the Oberkampf Kibbutz. Perhaps it is inevitable that a man from the Pampas of Argentina would find a compact Parisian space claustrophobic. But for me after a lifetime of "expat-class" houses (immense spaces behind high walls) in the developing world, I have an aversion to big spaces and find our 635 square feet a perfectly cozy nest.

"Are you ready kids?" I shout.

"Who is taking me?" Lorenzo asks. He has his shirt on backwards and his jeans are unbuttoned. "You or Pop?"

Pop, short for Papa, is what the kids call Tano. Although he finds it completely normal that his children call him this—he called his own father Papi—I find it totally endearing, for not only is it a foreign variation on my "Daddy," the shortened "Pop" makes me think of 1950s America, like something one would hear in an old sitcom like *Happy Days*.

"Pop is taking you," I say, getting his shirt turned the right way and buttoning his pants. When Lorenzo's shoes are on and tied in double knots, I kiss all three of my family members goodbye. Then I down a last quick coffee, and race for the metro.

Throughout the day I listen to my clients' dilemmas, all the while trying to manage my own anxiety. Tano is determined to convince me that Lyon is great, but all I can think about are African war zones, rickety charter planes, dangerous roads, and disease—all elements he contends with regularly in his work with MSF. The possibility of something awful happening to him is a reality I have lived with all these years, and the only consolation has been having this stable home base in Paris where the kids and I stay while we wait for his safe return.

That evening when I get home, the kids are down in the courtyard with the assortment of other children that live in our building. How I would hate to leave this convivial community, where kids run freely throughout the building, popping into various apartments to get an extra ball or jump rope or prop for whatever game has broken out in the courtyard.

Tano waits for me upstairs, and before I even put my purse down he starts. "Why won't you even consider making this move?"

"What if we move to Lyon and then you die, Tano? The kids and I will be down there completely alone."

"I'm not going to die!"

"How the hell do you know?"

"The new job is a *desk* job. It has almost no risk. I've told you that."

"Well what if you leave me?" My voice cracks mid-sentence. There: I said it. All of those old trust issues I claimed to have dealt with so neatly years ago—*la di da, we're fine!*—come rushing to the surface, the stunning pain of betrayal, the affliction of jealousy and mistrust.

"*Leave* you?"

"Yeah, like for another woman." Just saying the words causes my heart to clench up like a fist and I realize: *I haven't really forgiven him; I haven't fully recovered.*

Tano looks stricken. "Is that what you think?" Before I can answer he pulls me to him and kisses me. "*Kreestin.*" That's all he says, my name, pronounced in his trilling Latin accent, with a tone that says I am crazy to imagine such a thing.

And while it does make me feel better, it isn't enough to make me change my mind, because I cannot, as it turns out, imagine our life outside of Paris, as though the city itself is the very glue that has been keeping us together. All I can think about is that if I follow Tano to Lyon I will have to trust in my marriage completely enough to let go of the independence I have found in Paris; to trust enough to be buoyed by the idea that he *would* take care of me, present and future, so that ensuring my own capacity to do so would never again feel so urgent.

I just can't do it.

And so Tano moves to Lyon without us.

Three

In more panicked moments, I worry that our new divided life will lead to the end of our marriage, upset as Tano is that I won't move with him, and upset as I am that he expects me to. But in fact, the debate about the separation, and the separation itself, *revives* it. Absence—and uncertainty—really does make the heart grow fonder—and certain other body parts, as well.

I call it the new marriage model: Two days on, five days off.

It's like having a fabulous new romance.

Friday evenings, Tano trains up to Paris from Lyon, arriving doting and intentional, wanting to know what I need help with before he has to go back late Sunday night. And I, unencumbered by the stresses and strains of a shared daily routine, receive him with an equal dose of uxorious attention. We rediscover a state of domestic bliss that feels remarkably like being newlyweds, where he attends to little household projects while I cook for him, each one of us playing out our gender assignments when the kids aren't clambering all over him.

And best of all?

Friday and Saturday nights, under the new marriage model we *also* clamber all over each other, like sex-crazed animals coming out of a long hibernation.

I love it all—being on my own with the kids during the week, an efficient single working mother, and on the weekends reuniting with my handsome Latino lover.

Tano clearly enjoys our new honeymoonish weekends as much as I do—the passionate kisses hello and good-bye don't lie—but he is the one who has to juggle two places, the one who is always on the go, the one who lives in a beautiful new city that he barely knows anything about because he has no time there to explore, and no one to explore with.

Never one to belabor a point, months go by where he doesn't say anything. But just when I start to think that he has really forgotten his agenda—or accepted mine—he brings it up again.

"So when are you joining me in Lyon?"

It is a Tuesday evening and we have been chatting on the phone for the last half hour. We are almost a year in to the Paris-Lyon arrangement by now, and it has been several weeks since the last time he raised the subject. I owe it to him to have the discussion, but why does he have to bring it up at bedtime?

"It's 11:45, Tano. Do we really have to talk about this right now?"

"Why not?"

I sigh. Of course he thinks it's a great time to talk, because down in Lyon on his own he has reverted to what I call "South American schedule," which basically means doing everything three to four hours later than what I consider normal. "Because I want to go to sleep."

This time it is Tano that sighs.

"What?" I say, torn between crabbiness and concern for the genuine despair the sound transmits.

"Are you trying to get rid of me?"

"Of course not!"

"Well it sure feels like it."

I know, even if he doesn't state it explicitly, that this is his unhealed wound from our long-ago breakup, when I took Carmen and left, and then hesitated and stalled before welcoming him back into my life. The fact that I had a rebound affair with his colleague while we were separated made our reconciliation that much more painful.

"Tano, I have an extremely fulfilling life here. I can't just leave it."

"But I *miss* you," he says. "I *miss* the kids. I'm a married man and a father, but I live alone."

I kick the covers off my feet, feeling myself tense up *and* weaken. How can I resist a man who laments my absence?

"I want a real life together," he goes on. "As a family. I want to take care of you. *All* of you."

He is inviting me to let go of my attachment to my professional life and my obsession with being financially independent; it's an expression of love, and I do appreciate it. But the memory of being stuck—without my own resources and the capacity to take care of myself or our children—seems to have marred me for life.

"Why can't you trust me?" Tano's voice breaks into my thoughts. "I'm *not* going to leave you. I'm *never* going to leave you. And I am trying to give our family the best life possible. But you're making it so hard."

And before I can even produce a rebuttal he adds, "So I guess you win."

HUH?

"I'll come back to Paris. I'll call Jean-François on Monday."

Jean-François was his boss at MSF in Paris.

Suddenly the future flashes before my eyes. No more fabulous weekend love affair with my husband. Tano is going to move back to Paris and install his big masculine body in the 635 square feet that feels oh-so-cozy for me alone with the kids, but cramped as hell, I have to admit, when shared on a full-time basis with a man whose teasing good nature incites their wildness.

My mind flips to soccer matches breaking out in the living room right as I am herding the kids to bed, guitar ballads, lovely as they are, at midnight when I want to sleep, and other old domestic infractions that more often than not spring from our cultural differences.

Not to mention, my thoughts race, *bye bye great new salary*— the one that we now rely on for the material pleasures—dinners, movies, outings—that were an infrequent occurrence when we squeaked by on his modest MSF income.

Shit.

I sit up in bed, suddenly wide awake. "Wait!"

"I can't wait any longer."

"I'll move to Lyon."

Oh, Jesus. Did I really say that? I look wildly around my little bedroom, half expecting to see a ventriloquist in the corner.

Tano is as surprised. "Really?"

"I guess so," I stammer.

"You'll do that for me?"

His voice is so grateful, so *touched*—he clearly understands what a stretch this is for me—that I feel moved, too. Magnanimous, even, in spite of my impulsive change of tune. "This summer. We'll let the kids finish up the school year."

"Good," he says. "I've already got a quote from a moving company."

So, he knew I'd cave all along.

"And we can get the apartment valued and on the market next month."

"*What?* No way are we selling the apartment."

"But we won't need it anymore. We're *leaving.*"

I am too choked up to speak, my mind hurtling back over the years to so many departure scenes from my childhood. When we left a post, it was always permanent, facilitated by the fact that the US Embassy provided our housing every time. In my much younger years, our departures included histrionic acts of vandalism by me and my sisters: snipping pieces of the Embassy-issue rugs and sofa coverings, our childish attempts to take something with us, some physical proof of an existence that we knew we would never return to.

Now, twenty-five years later, I will not endure the same scenario. We *won't* always have Paris if we let go of the one thing we possess, the 635 square feet on rue Oberkampf where we will always have a right and a reason to come home to.

"Selling the apartment will be like cutting off our feet," I finally say. *Or cutting out my heart.*

"Isn't that a bit melodramatic?"

I am suddenly offended, by his insistence, his pragmatism. I *know* that holding on to our apartment will have a major impact on our children's sense of stability as they grow up. How can Tano understand? He has *his* place—that small city in central Argentina where he knows everyone and his siblings and mother and aunts and cousins all live within half a mile of each other. His entire life history is still solidly available to him. I know that if we don't have a place to go back to—and crashing on friends' sofas doesn't count—Paris cannot continue to exist in the same way for us.

"We *need* a base," I say. "*I* need a base. And I refuse to sell this apartment."

Now it is half past midnight, which is getting late even for Tano, so he drops the subject, but not before saying, "I just can't wait until we all live together again."

We hang up and I try to read a few pages to calm down, but I cannot concentrate, feeling shaky and emotional and possessed by one thought: *What have I done?*

I've agreed to yank off my life as though it is a shirt grown too old, and not the secure, warm cloak that I know it to be. *Paris, my love*, I cry inside my head. *I cannot bear to leave you.*

I toss and turn all night long, feeling an awful sense of angst, as though I am being torn between two lovers. Paris and Lyon. Or is it Paris and Tano?

Why, oh *why*, do I have to choose?

Already I mourn the loss of this solid, concrete life. I fear the eventual end of my relationships and the unqualified easiness of our shared existence. People change in your absence, they forget about you or fill your place at the table with someone more readily available. I haven't even left yet but I already miss so many people: Friends, neighbors, colleagues, clients... I see them all disappearing from my life forever.

Somewhere inside me leaving still means losing.

Four

The decision to move may have been made, but how to *tell* people? After months of indignant speeches—*Can you believe he thinks I'm going to move?*—now I have to admit that I've agreed to it.

So much for taking a stand.

The first people I inform are my family back in the States. I am not surprised that my parents and sisters are in full support of the plan. They have been well aware of my resistance to leaving Paris, but they are also well aware of our small apartment and tight economic situation, at least before Tano changed jobs. His new job allows him to earn more than triple of what I generate as a self-employed therapist, and knowing this, my family has said, directly and indirectly, that it would be crazy for me to strong-arm him into giving it up.

Here in Paris, though, I don't know how to tell my nearest and dearest. I sit on it for a few days until I text Susan and George, my Scottish neighbors on the first floor. This couple and their son, Matthew, have become our extended family in Paris, fellow foreigners floating along in a French ocean.

Susan answers immediately: *This is the worst news of my year. Pop down for a glass of wine when you can. XXX*

Then I call Deanna, another of my closest friends in Paris. The phone goes straight to her voicemail so I leave a message: *Hi D, Big news. Need to talk to you ASAP. Call me.*

Deanna is also an American therapist, from the Chicago suburbs, who started a new life in Paris when she married her French boyfriend, Regis. She gave up a twenty-year career working with kids and teens when she came to France. We met at a networking gig shortly after we'd both arrived and hit it off over a shared love of disco music and the challenge of launching our private practices in France.

We rented our very first—and very tiny—office in a pretty little building on a cobblestone street right off the Champ de Mars in the seventh *arrondissement*. Quickly, we were both busy enough to need our own spaces, so Deanna moved into an office right above the one we had shared.

Since then, we have been in near-constant contact, chatting between clients and having beginning and end-of-day check-ins. So I find it strange that a full day goes by and she doesn't call me back. Her silence seems providential: is the end already in sight, before I have even announced my departure? My rational brain knows this is an extreme reaction, but the "I'm moving blues" have set in, and all relationships seem fragile to me when threatened by geography.

But I am dying to talk to Deanna. I need her advice. How am I supposed to approach the termination process with my clients?

I care deeply about the people I work with, and dread telling them that I am leaving. As I enter the courtyard of our office building my head is full of the good-bye scenarios I will soon face: *seventeen-year-old Mia who recently lost her mother in a car accident; Alexandra, who is having an affair with a married man; Jane, a high-powered businesswoman who gave up her career in pharmaceuticals eighteen months ago to follow her husband to Paris, convinced she'd land on her feet—now still jobless and extremely depressed. Martha, whose husband left her after twenty-five years of marriage.*

Oh God, I think, as the details of Martha's situation flood my brain: she trailed him around the world for years, piecing odd jobs together. Now he's trying to skimp on alimony and she has nothing to fall back on, no retirement to speak of, and no home base to return to… Panic about what I have just agreed to mounts, but then I see Deanna. She stands in front of my door, a strange expression on her face.

"I found a lump in my breast."

I am so startled by her statement that I have to ask her to repeat it.

"A lump. In my breast."

In the privacy of my office she lifts her shirt. "I mean, this *is* a lump, isn't it?" She guides my fingers to the mass. It feels *huge.* Our eyes lock. Then she says, "I couldn't get an appointment until Friday."

"*Friday?*" I make no effort to disguise my mounting hysteria.

My natural inclination is never to assume that everything is going to be all right, especially when it comes to matters of death and dying. Deanna knows this about me.

"It might be nothing," Deanna says. Still, she prods some more, and her tone betrays her doubt. "Let's change the subject. Tell me something, anything, to take my mind off of this. Make something up if you need to."

"No need to make things up," I say. She's provided the perfect segue. "I caved in. I agreed to move to Lyon."

Five

That evening I call Tano, in tears. "Deanna has a lump!"

"A lump of what?"

I fill him in on the details.

"Hopefully it's just something benign," he says. "But if not, at least she gets excellent health care here."

"I don't think I should move, Tano. What if she's ill?"

"You're getting ahead of yourself, Querida. And even if she is, you'll only be two hours away."

I can't bear to tell him that Deanna's lump has made me think: What if we move to Lyon and then *I* find some horrible lump?

But Tano knows me too well. "*You* do not have cancer, Querida."

"How do you know?"

"Because I know."

My mind flashes back five years to when Carmen was seven and Lorenzo was one, and I discovered that the ugly mole on my face was a stage two melanoma. The cancer was excised, leaving a three-inch scar running down the left side of my face and a horrific, tentacular, death anxiety. I took a short course of Lexomil, a Valium derivative distributed like Halloween candy in France, but it made me so sleepy I couldn't use it and still function. Instead I got into therapy—sort of.

My "therapist" was Dr. Bernard Michel, a melanoma specialist at Hôpital Saint Louis, one of the most prestigious cancer hospitals in France. Dr. Michel identified me immediately as a *patiente très anxieuse*—I saw it scribbled in my chart—and I suspect this is why he always divided our appointments into two parts: one for my weepy outpourings, the other for the skin examination. I could clearly use some of that brand of therapy right now, so as soon as I get off the phone with Tano, I call Dr. Michel's answering service and request an emergency rendezvous. Amazingly, a spot is available the following evening.

Twenty-four hours later, I sit before Dr. Michel. With his lithe form, usually clad in jeans, a plaid shirt, and hiking boots, he looks more like a handsome park ranger than a skin cancer specialist. Truthfully, I am totally in love with him. Now I wring my hands and tell him about Deanna, moving to Lyon, and that the combined anxiety of these two developments have triggered a hypochondriacal panic attack: If I move the melanoma will come back!

"*Ne vous inquiétez pas, Madame,*" he consoles, his voice so gentle he could teach guided meditation. "*Vous avez le droit de guérir.*"

Don't worry, Madame. You have the right to recover.

What "right" is he referring to, exactly?

"Try telling that to some aggressive cancer cell that would be thrilled to take me down," I say.

He laughs. "What is it you are really afraid of, Madame? Assuming you don't die first from melanoma?"

I chew on my fingernail for a moment. "That I'll leave Paris and then my marriage will fall apart again and I'll have nothing left."

He looks contemplative. "Do you *have* to move?"

I explain how if I don't move to Lyon, Tano will move back to Paris, and how in spite of having resisted this for so long, part of me feels that it was inevitable that I'd *have* to go wherever Tano worked. Maybe because as a child those issues had always been dictated by my parents—with no room for debate.

"But now you are an adult," he muses. "And you do have decision-making power."

"Well I did put my foot down about selling our apartment."

"*Très bien,*" he affirms. "And what else do you need to feel secure?"

The answer is simple: my own money.

"Then why don't you keep your practice open a few days a week?" Dr. Michel says. "Lots of medical professionals divide their time between locations."

His suggestion is so offhand, so casual, I cannot believe that something that obvious had not already occurred to me. "That's a great idea," I say, pushing away the one thought that flares up in opposition: *If I commute I will have to leave the children, and I have never really been away from them with any regularity.*

He shrugs and puts down his magnifying lens. "You have to organize your life in a way that makes sense to you."

Indeed. Still, I wonder how Tano will feel about this idea. It will be a total role reversal. He is the designated traveler in the marriage, not me. And though I have gotten really good at saying no, sometimes a simple "no" is easier than completing the sentence: *I want…*

Six

On Friday, Deanna's doctor performs a needle biopsy that leaves her breast bruised and tender. A few hours later the verdict comes in: It's cancer.

Deanna has breast cancer.

Oh my fucking God.

We are stunned, scared, and we cancel all of our afternoon appointments to sit together on the sofa of her office. *I just can't believe it,* we say, and *Now what? What the hell happens next?*

There are doctors' appointments to make and follow-up ultrasounds and blood work and in the midst of all of this Deanna's phone keeps ringing. A client needs an emergency appointment. Another one wants to change her appointment time.

"I cannot take the stress," Deanna says. The look on her face tells me that her whole life is flashing before her eyes.

"What do you want to do about work?" I ask. This may seem an odd question given everything that she is absorbing, but I know how hard it is to be "on" as a therapist when your own life has been so shaken.

"I need to take a break. I feel so anxious I don't think I can be present with anyone." Her tears fall. "It's like a preparation for death."

I throw my arms around her and we cry together. Deanna is not the type to fall for platitudes like, "it's gonna be okay," and "we're gonna win this battle." Instead I say, "This really fucking sucks."

After a moment she reaches for a tissue and blows her nose. "Well, we started out together, I guess we get to wrap it all up together."

She is referring to relinquishing our hard-earned professional existences. Although the scale of what we are dealing with is incomparable, really, the end result is the type of professional death that a self-employed person faces by removing themselves from the playing field. The most critical part of building a successful therapy practice is developing a presence, a reputation, in a community. It's a competitive field, and suddenly being unavailable means passing rapidly to oblivion.

I am about to tell her that I am thinking of only bowing out halfway, and maybe it would be good for her spirits, too, to keep a few office hours open per week, but suddenly the phone rings again. It is Regis, proposing that they go away for the weekend. She doesn't begin chemo for another week, and he thinks it would be good to get their minds off what's ahead.

His voice carries through the receiver and into Deanna's office.

"Let's go to Lyon," he says. Regis once lived there and has already told Deanna that it's a fabulous city and that I am crazy for stalling.

Lyon as a getaway from cancer. Instantly I feel ashamed. Talk about getting some perspective.

A few hours later I call Tano and catch him right before he boards the TGV train for Paris.

"Look for Deanna and Regis," I say, and then, trying to sound offhand, although I have been practicing since my appointment with Dr. Michel, "I can't bear to fold up my practice, Tano."

I hear his breath hitch. "Are you backing out of the move?"

"No. But I want... I want..."

"Yes?"

"I want to commute. I've thought it over and I want to spend two days per week in Paris."

"That will be very hectic."

"But it will allow me to keep my practice alive."

"Until you get a new practice established in Lyon?"

"Of course," I say, although I have given almost no thought to what I might pull together for myself in Lyon.

"Okay," he sighs. "Whatever you think is the right way for you to do this."

I have prepared a longer series of justifications, expecting more of an argument and am amazed that he has just agreed. "Look for Deanna," I say again.

My relief blinds me to the reality that their trains will be speeding too fast in opposite directions to even wave from the window.

Seven

The French school year is divided up by interminable school holidays. School always starts the first week of September, then, toward the end of October the kids get two weeks off. They get two more weeks at Christmas, two more in February, and then another two in March/April, depending on when Easter falls. There are four long weekends in May, and then most of July and all of August, not to mention *les grèves*—strikes—that every year, at any given moment, shut the schools down from one day to the next, putting working parents into the same conundrum: What to do with the kids?

These incessant holidays and shutdowns provide a constant reminder of our foreign status here in France, for every time the schools close for more than a day, most of the French kids we know disappear to houses elsewhere that have been in their family for generations, accompanied by gaggles of cousins and *TaTas* and *TonTons* (aunts and uncles) and *Mamies* and *Papis* (Grandmas and Grandpas). Even the kids whose parents blithely reject material wealth, expressing their *solidarité* with the underclass of France, seem to take every school holiday at some idyllic seaside cove or rural haven with doting extended families all around them. I am sorely jealous, as our kids' holidays are always patched together: a few days of *centre de loisirs* (day camp, held in the cafeteria of their school), a few days at Susan and George's, and a few days with me who always takes days off work to cover the bases.

In late January, Carmen and Lorenzo have already asked what they will be doing during *les vacances de février*—the February holidays. All their school friends are talking about upcoming ski trips to the mountains.

"Would you like to go visit Pop in Lyon?"

"Yes!" Carmen enthuses. "It's like we have a vacation house, too!"

We'll see about that, I think, envisioning the four of us crammed into his 200-square-feet studio. But I let her dwell in her fantasy. We won't be spending a lot of time in the apartment because we have a mission to accomplish: figuring out where to live come summer.

The task is both exciting and daunting, and I can't help compare the process to all the moves my family made with the Foreign Service when I was a child, long before e-mail or the Internet. God, it was so much easier. Washington assigned us to a house in the vicinity of the Embassy and the international school, and that was it.

With the housing assignment we received the Post Report, a fifteen-page document that explained a few things about the country we'd be moving to and a lot more about the post itself: Where would we do our food shopping? What did the community do on the weekends? Was the post safe?

Closer to our arrival date, my father would receive a cable telling us who would be our sponsor, an Embassy family already at post that would arrange to have groceries in the house upon our arrival, take us around the city on an orientation tour, have us over for dinner, induct us into our new lives.

It was all neatly packaged.

Lyon will be my fourth major move with Tano—and the fourth time we have to go it alone. We have never had a Post Report, a welcoming committee, and a neat little dossier to study before we even land. Once again, Tano and I are on our own to organize our new lives, a task that has already degenerated into argument because Tano's idea is to get a house with a garden in the rural suburbs.

"*The rural suburbs?*"

Although I am clearly aghast, he insists that it makes no sense to move to a city known for its beautiful environs, and live in the urban center.

"But if we live in the suburbs we'll have to *drive* everywhere."

We, who have not owned a car since we left East Africa ten years earlier and who can't consider getting one as we don't have French driver's licenses. (For the record: We both have tons of driving experience and valid licenses from our respective countries. But in France you don't just pass a test and "get" a license. Unless you exchange your foreign license in the first year you live here, assuming you even have a license from a country France is willing to swap with, you have to attend driving school. In France this is a notoriously expensive and crookedly fail-happy system.)

Without French driver's licenses we cannot get a car, and without a car there is no way we can live in the rural suburbs, and this suits me just fine as that very scenario cuts straight to my angst of losing all the independence that a pedestrian, urban existence has provided.

So the February holidays are designated as the first step in figuring out this new Lyonnais life. It is therapeutic to do the research about our move as a family, for the kids to be involved. At least that's what I've been telling all the Parents' Groups I've worked with in Paris for almost a decade.

Not that Carmen seems to need any therapizing at this point, as she is already over the moon that Lyon's more permissive cost of living means that for the first time since her little brother arrived on the scene six years ago, she will have her own bedroom. I have also promised that we can adopt two kittens once we are settled.

Her eyes shine and her voice takes on this soft, dreamy quality. "Kittens. My dream come true."

For Lorenzo the conversation about finding a new place to live is less clear-cut. He doesn't seem to understand that when we talk about bigger apartments and kittens and new schools that it isn't a game of hypotheticals.

"Those are things to have at Lyon?" he says in his husky voice. "I prefer to have them at Paris."

The poignancy of his statement prevents me from applying what I have learned about correcting the linguistic mistakes of bilingual children. (Without making a big deal of it, I am supposed to play a corrected version of his sentence back to him: Those are things we'll have *in* Lyon, not *in* Paris, darling.)

His expressed preference for Paris touches me, but I am not too worried. Carmen, my pre-teen, is the one I need to keep a close eye on. She is heading toward adolescence, after all, and teenagers are developmentally so busy individuating from their parents, so identified with their peers, that uprooting them can feel like Armageddon.

I weave these thoughts into a talk I give at one of the international schools in Paris one evening, right before the school holidays. I give this particular talk—*Raising Global and Mobile Children: Challenges and Solutions for International Families*— about three times a year and the room is always packed. Usually when I introduce myself I talk about growing up as an Embassy kid, and how that influenced my desire to work as a therapist with internationally mobile families. I explain how a traveling childhood can influence children of the same family in entirely different ways. My family of origin is a great example. While my elder sister, Lesley, also became a trailing spouse, following her military husband around the United States, my younger sister, Steph moved to small town Maryland from Jakarta, Indonesia and never left again!

Tonight I also build in some storytelling about how I am in the midst of moving my own children.

"It's much easier to move younger kids," I say, "because younger kids are still more attached to their families than to their exterior worlds."

The members of the audience are nodding their heads and taking notes. I talk about the importance of saying proper good-byes to the places we leave behind, and the value in creating routines and rituals in the new place, as a child's sense of personal stability will come, at least in part, from feelings of familiarity. "So if you can identify a favorite place in your new country—a park, a pool, a library, a restaurant—go back to that place frequently," I say. "It will help your kids feel connected, at home."

Then it's question-and-answer time, and someone asks me if there is any "best-odds" recipe for moving kids.

I reiterate some of what we have already discussed. "But unfortunately, no," I add, "there is no 'recipe' for moving perfectly. It's always going to be a bit of a crapshoot."

What I don't say is that I can still feel my own childhood jitters about new cities and new schools tingle inside me: a perfect mix of thrill and dread. I had once thought that this was what my own children would never know, for I wanted to give them what Tano has—a pure sense of belonging to place. Part of me feels like I am making a huge mistake uprooting them, but another part of me knows that there are no mistakes, just experiences. And it occurs to me that my children's childhoods, which thus far have played out quite differently from mine in terms of geographic stability, have just been transformed into something that resembles my own. This is the first time that their lives will take the twist that defined my formative years—*being new*—and the best I can do right now is keep an eye on them both and respond to things as they come up.

Eight

The day after school closes for the two-week holiday, Carmen, Lorenzo and I board the TGV at Paris's Gare de Lyon. Two hours later, after traveling three hundred miles per hour through the frost-covered plains of Burgundy, our train pulls to an impatient halt at Lyon's Gare Part-Dieu.

Tano has come to meet us and after a quick tour of his little studio that sits minutes from the quai du Rhône, a pedestrian and cycling path that runs along the river, we go out to explore the city. The day is beaming with sun and I cannot believe how much Lyon diverges from my Parisian template. Comparatively, it is so sporty, like a French San Diego. All the years I have lived in Paris I have never seen so many people in spandex.

We head north along the river, which is lined with bars and houseboats. A family of winter birds crosses the bike path as Tano leads us up the ramp to the street where we reach the golden gates of the Tête d'Or. It is a 290-acre park—the biggest urban park in France—with running trails, a lake with paddleboats and ducks, even a zoo.

We spend the rest of the afternoon meandering through the Tête d'Or, and Tano remarks that since I've vetoed the suburbs, it would be nice to live nearby. Imagine being able to just pop out of the apartment and be in the midst of all this green!

The neighborhood around the park really is lovely with its tree-lined sidewalks and view of the Rhône, but all the buildings seem so *modern*. I still believe, even after all these years in France, that one of the very reasons for living here is to live in something old. Sagging floors and dilapidated staircases take on a different meaning when you think of some French peasant toiling there four hundred years earlier.

I express this sentiment the next day, when we are strolling through Vieux Lyon, the Old Town. This area is nestled into a spot between the banks of the Saône River and the foot of a hill called Fourvière, after the majestic basilica that sits atop it, presiding over the city.

"I doubt any peasant ever lived in the kinds of buildings you are interested in living in," Tano says.

He thinks I am a prima donna, for when we peruse the rental ads my eyes go immediately to the apartments that are totally out of our budget. I ignore his comment and point out something I have already gathered in these couple of days of running around: Lyon is so much smaller than Paris, we don't actually have to live near the park. Compared to the Parisian scale of things, no matter where we live in Lyon, we *will* be "near" it. And if we did live on the (nearby) other side of town, the city is super easy to traverse by foot or by public transport (which, incidentally, is much nicer than in Paris: Pleasant tunes are piped into the Lyonnais metro station, and the trains themselves are clean and don't stink like a bag of throw-up and farts. There are even platform attendants to help manage the crowds getting on and off).

Monday morning at 8:30 a.m., a bleary-eyed Tano speeds off to work along the quai du Rhône on the fabulous racing bike he has invested in to get himself around the city. Now that the kids and I are in Lyon he is back on North American schedule, not that his new "early" bedtime at midnight makes his 7:30 wake up any easier. Once he is gone, I rally the kids to get their shoes on so that we can eat a picnic breakfast of warm *pain au chocolat* down on the quai. At this hour, the path along the river is quiet, the only sounds the *spat-puff spat-puff spat-puff* of the runners, their shoes against pavement, their quick breaths mixed in with the occasional whirl of a biker's wheels. The benches lining the quai host a few couples, asleep in each other's arms, their nightclub garb from the evening before out of place in the watery light.

When we are done eating, the kids and I cross what will become one of our favorite bridges, the Passerelle du Collège. Of the thirty bridges that cross the two rivers in Lyon, this is one of the few pedestrian walkways. It takes us right into the funky end of Lyon's city center, situated on the Presqu'île—"almost-island"—the peninsula that lies in between the two rivers.

Most days we repeat this routine, just eating a quick sandwich for lunch while we watch the skateboarders around Hôtel de Ville—the town hall. But one day it is particularly cold, and so we take a table under a heat lamp at a café. We face the fountain on place des Terreaux, where four fired-up horses pull the Carriage of Liberty.

"So what do you think, kids?" I ask. "Do you think you'll enjoy living in Lyon?"

"Totally," Carmen says. She reaches down to touch the shopping bag tucked between our two chairs. Inside is the cool T-shirt I have just bought her at a trendy art store.

Lorenzo doesn't seem to be listening; he's mesmerized by the band of teenagers whizzing by on skateboards and the *CRACK!* of wheels and wood as they smack back to the pavement. They land so hard, with such *vitesse*, it's a wonder they don't snap their kneecaps.

"Lyon is pretty cool, isn't it, Zozos?" I say, using the name that he gave himself, years ago, when he was first learning to speak. Only recently, when he turned five, did he say he wanted us to stop calling him such a "babyish" name. Today he is oblivious. He shrugs and turns back to the skaters. "It's okay."

I give him a little squeeze and ask if he'd like to get his own skateboard. He skates regularly in the courtyard of the Oberkampf kibbutz, using the old board of a neighbor.

"I can get my very own skateboard?"

"You can, my love. Once we've moved here."

He thinks about it for a moment. "That's okay," he finally says. "I'll just stay at Paris instead."

So bribery is not going to work.

Then he says, "Mom, can we go to that Paris part of Lyon?"

At first I am confused. Then I realize what he's talking about: the area of the city south of the Musée des Beaux Arts. The little streets that meander around the Hôtel de Ville open up in to broader swaths of avenue lined with buildings that have a unified aspect to their facades, much like the *Haussmannienne* architecture that characterizes so much of Paris.

I agree, and we make our way. The further south we go the funky street culture seems to fall away until it disappears completely, as the passersby go from chic to downright dripping with wealth. We literally gape when a woman in a tight white suit, high-heeled tennis shoes, and a feather boa struts by with the head of a little poodle, completely relaxed, hanging out of her handbag.

We turn up an old gray stone street, flanked by meticulous clothing shops and artsy boutiques. Lorenzo wants to admire an elegant display of samurai swords in a gallery window but we are summoned by Carmen who shouts, "Mom! Lorenzo! Quick!"

She has stopped in front of a *pâtisserie* called Pignol. It is clear from the serious culinary garb of the employees inside and the stunning rows of pastries that the establishment has earned its reputation as one of the finest pâtisseries in France—or so says a newspaper clipping in the window. We drool at the display for just a moment. Then we go in.

The attendant greets us with crisp professionalism. "*Vous désirez, Madame?*"

I tell him we need more time to decide.

"Perhaps you have come for *une tarte écossaise?*"

In the moment I think he suggests the "Scottish tart" because my accent has misled him. But then he says, "*C'est notre specialité.*"

Well if it's their specialty than we've got to try it, *n'est-ce pas?*

I propose that we choose several things to share, and we settle on the *tarte écossaise,* a *framboisier,* a *millefeuille,* and an *éclair au chocolat.* Monsieur arranges them into a box and with a few fussy twists of the wrist, a snap of tape and ribbon, we emerge from the shop with a beautiful little package.

We cross the street to place Bellecour with our treats. Had I read the guidebook I've been lugging around, I might have realized that our pig-out is about to be staged at the third largest square in all of France. But alas, I had not done my research, and probably never would have if Lorenzo had not asked if the statue of some fellow on horseback trotting across the plaza, with naked women and lions draped at his feet, was the Lone Ranger.

I dig out the guidebook.

"Actually, darling, it's Louis the 14th."

Apparently the statue was destroyed during the French Revolution, and only recreated in 1825. Today it appears to be the meeting point of people of all ages: grandmothers pushing strollers, middle-aged couples resting their feet, a group of Japanese tourists having a picnic in its shadow. Lorenzo joins the group of kids who are climbing all over the naked women, and Carmen joins ranks with the other tweens and teens who huddle in groups on the steps leading up to the statue, smoking cigarettes and texting.

I lean back on my elbows and soak up the scene. How strange to think that one day this might not feel like unknown territory. I open the pastry box, and look over to Carmen and Lorenzo. Neither of them makes eye contact, and I really don't want to shout, but oh man I am dying to try one of these little delicacies.

The tarte écossaise sits so innocently in the box. It is a beautiful, compact little cake, although not one I would have chosen had I not been informed that it is Pignol's specialty. I am generally drawn to the other type of pastry we bought: the ones that look fancy and extravagant, kind of like the apartments that Tano mocks me for drooling over. The tarte écossaise, on the other hand, looks efficient, modest even, by comparison, with its perfectly round cookie-cutter shape, a thin layer of yellow glaze its only adornment.

The kids won't care if I eat this without them: they barely shrugged when I suggested we try it. I lift it from its little silver doily, surprised by its weight.

The first bite takes me: Sweet lord it is SO GOOD.

It is like a moist shortbread and that yellow glaze is so fruity, so flavorful. I examine the inside of the tarte through the crescent-shaped teeth tracks that bear a sheen of my drool. Pure butter and almonds with just a dash of flour and sugar to hold it together.

In another two bites it is gone.

The kids are still completely oblivious to my attempts to make eye contact, so without waiting I pick out the millefeuille.
Oh YUM.

Cold, sweet, creamy filling oozes onto my tongue from between paper thin layers of pastry.
Mmmmmmmmmm.

My teeth bite in again and the millefeuille literally melts in my mouth, this *ooooze* of goopy custardy cream following the first taste of this chewy sweet layer of icing sugar…

The screams of a child who has skinned his knees brings me back to the present. Place Bellecour, Lyon. France. Oh, no. I ate the whole millefeuille! I look over at the kids. Lorenzo seems to be having a ball, climbing up and then propelling himself off the lion.

And Carmen is…chatting with a *boy?*

I grab the framboisier and take a big chomp.

Oh dear *God*. Cold, sweet cream, both dense and fluffy at the same time. How do they do that?

I demolish it in four gluttonous inhalations. Then I look back at Carmen. If that boy is trying to pick her up I guess I don't have to be too worried. He looks like he's about nine years old to her twelve.

I am about to reach for the éclair but suddenly Lorenzo stands before me, hands planted on his hips. "Mom!"

"Yes?"

"Where's the millefeuille?"

"Uhhhh...."

"Did you *eat* it?"

"Ummm...."

"And what about the framboisier? And the tarte écossaise?"

"Well, you see I tried to call you and Car—"

"Mom!" He stomps off about three feet away, sits down, puts his head in his hands and *cries*.

I feel like a total heel.

Carmen runs to him. "What's wrong, Lorenzo?"

Next thing I know she is in front of me. "Mom! How could you?"

"You didn't have to leave your conversation with that—"

"You're such a pig! You said we were going to share!"

"I saved the éclair," I say, sheepishly, although what I am thinking is that I *am* a pig. What kind of mother snarfs down the cake while her kids aren't looking?

I make it up to them by dividing the éclair into two (but not before sneaking a little taste) and then, when the kids have eaten their portions, we march straight back to Pignol. I even confess to the gentleman in the lab coat that we are back so soon because I lost control of myself (a detail he finds entirely uninteresting). We order another framboisier and another millefeuille—I was right, they don't really want the tarte écossaise—and the kids eat them at a table right there in the shop.

Lorenzo shakes his head in wonder. "I can't believe you didn't *share*, Mom."

"Yeah," Carmen says. "Do you have any idea what it's like when your mother eats all your cake?"

In fact, I do know that feeling. I remember vividly a night in London when I was nine years old. We were there en route to our posting in the Ivory Coast, and for whatever reason, that day my parents let each one of us kids choose a bag of candy—normally contraband in our household—to take back to the hotel.

I chose a bag of peanut M&M's. I can still remember how the paper of the bag felt, crisp and crinkling in my hand, and my mother gently lifting it from me—*if you keep fondling it that way you'll melt the chocolate!*—to keep safe in her purse.

I was excited about those M&M's because they were chocolate and chocolate was forbidden and the whole situation was kind of like what I was trying to do when I offered Lorenzo his very own skateboard. Nine-year-old me had taken the offer of those M&M's as an acknowledgment, somehow, of the fact that being on our way to West Africa was a big enough deal that I would be given something special to mark the event.

We were going to get back to that musty London hotel and watch television and eat our treats and it was going to be great.

But I had such terrible jetlag, and next thing I knew it was morning and I had slept through the TV watching and there, in the metal trashcan next to the desk in that frowzy hotel with the flowered curtains, was my empty M&M's packet.

Everyone else was still asleep when I made this discovery, but I made no attempt to contain my despair.

Me: Who did this?

My mother: Shhhhhh! You're going to wake your sisters!

Me: (low, devastated howl) But who ate *my* M&M's?

My mother: (long pause) Me.

Me: (full-on weeping) How could you, Mom?

My mother: (Sigh)

Me: Answer me!

My mother: You were asleep. And I needed a little treat, too.

At the time, her answer seemed infuriatingly inadequate. How could she have robbed me of something I was so looking forward to? On the shelf the M&M's were simply contraband; in my hand, they had taken on a magical quality, some protective shield between me and the anxiety I was already feeling about this move across continents.

Oh God. Was it possible that my own kids felt this way about the cakes from Pignol? Had I just wolfed down their entire sense of safety and self-confidence?

That night I lie in bed thinking about my mother. Carmen and Lorenzo's reaction this afternoon steered me back to my childhood, and I suddenly wonder what my own mom had been going through in that London hotel so many years ago. It never occurred to me to question the family narrative as I understood it—that moving across the world to West Africa was an adventure we *all* wanted. Was it possible that my mother had gobbled up my M&M's because she had dreaded going?

Fifteen years earlier, after I'd followed Tano to Kenya and *then* realized that I had signed up for a style of life that I did not want, I felt some vague feeling of alliance with my mother, a sense of parallel fatedness, as if through DNA itself I had inherited the struggle with dependency and identity. Once settled in Paris, this sense of connectedness to my own mother's story had fallen more into the backdrop. And though I had never asked how she'd felt about making the move before we ever left the United States, I remember distinctly asking her, right after Carmen was born, if in hindsight she ever wished we had never left.

"Well if *we* hadn't left maybe you would not have signed up to live abroad as an adult, and then I could see this beautiful baby as much as I want," she said, without missing a beat.

And then, no more. She may have offered something further if I had not changed the topic as quickly as possible. Though it was the only time I heard my mother acknowledge how my international childhood may have influenced certain choices I made as an adult, I generally steered clear of the topic because I felt guilty for living so far away.

Thinking about this always makes me feel anxious, so I have to tell myself to calm down, focusing on the soft, dreamy breaths of my family lying next to me. Finally I drift off, but sleep brings no solace, for I find myself in a horrific nightmare: my kids are locked in a room and a gnashing rat is chasing them. I can hear them screaming, "Mommy! Mommy!" But I cannot find the key. I have no purse, no pockets; in fact, I can't even move. Then, in the dream, I realize, this is not a door separating me from my kids, it is a coffin, in which I am buried. I am *dead*, no more, gone.

I startle awake with a shriek, shaking Tano, tears on my cheeks. "*Anything* could happen. Isn't that reason enough to just sit tight in Paris?"

He rubs my back to soothe me, with deep calm, that thing I so love about my husband, radiating from him. "Yes," he counters, "Anything *could* happen. Isn't that the very reason to try something new?"

Nine

In France it is extremely difficult—impossible, even—for an owner to evict a renter from their property, even if the renter has stopped paying rent. We have heard horror stories of people paying heavy mortgages on properties that have been taken over by delinquent renters who stay year after year, rent free, protected by the legal system. This extreme protection of the renter falls under *la loi Alur*, which in my mind sounds fittingly – for the corrupt or insolvent renter, that is—like "the alluring law."

Given my utter terror of getting an unevictable squatter in my beloved cozy nest, I decide that the only people I can trust to move into our apartment are people that have full-fledged lives elsewhere.

In other words, people on sabbatical.

And because the dimensions of our life are about to change dramatically, it seems obvious that we just leave all the furniture sized for the 635 square feet—the love seat-sized couch, the four-seater dining table, the college-dorm-size half fridge—in Paris, and re-outfit our material lives from scratch once we have arrived in Lyon.

I list our apartment in the Oberkampf kibbutz on sabbaticalhomes.com:

635 square feet, Quartier Oberkampf, comes fully furnished with Internet, electricity, and the owner, who will be there maximum two nights per week.

Tano flips when he sees the announcement. "You're renting out the apartment with *you* in it? What kind of deal is that?"

To me it makes perfect sense. I am going to be in Paris two days per week anyway for work. Susan and George have already extended their "door is always open" policy. But I can't leave Paris, rent out my pad, and then freeload down on the first floor. The most obvious arrangement seems to be renting our two-bedroom as a one bedroom, and keeping one of the rooms for myself.

But this brilliant ploy to let-go-without-really-letting-go falls apart for a variety of reasons. The first comes in an unexpected show of support for the trailing spouse from *Monsieur le tax collector*. Apparently, any expenses I accrue while back in Paris for work—such as hotel and restaurant—can be considered a business deduction, since it isn't my "fault" that my husband has taken a job elsewhere, forcing me to move far away from my professional activity. If I stay in my own apartment, however, I won't be able to claim any deduction.

"Nor will we be able to collect a full rent from anyone that has to be roommates with you," Tano points out, sternly.

Reluctantly I change the text of the ad:

635 square feet, Quartier Oberkampf, looking for a family who will love our home as though it is their own.

Almost immediately I make contact with a professor from Kent State University, who is looking for a two-bedroom apartment for himself, his wife, and his ten-year-old daughter. He is so earnest about finding a good place for his family—a real *home*, he writes—that in a flash I know that they are "the ones," and all I want to do is move them in and make them the guardians of our ghosts.

I rent the apartment—without me in it—to the Kent State family. But as soon as the lease is signed, I feel jittery. If our spot in the Oberkampf kibbutz is occupied, we really *are* leaving.

In a fit of panic I call Tano. "The lease is signed. We've got to move fast."

"Why? It's not even April yet. You're not moving down here until July."

"What if we have problems finding a place?"

"We won't."

But the idea of leaving our home in Paris and being stuck, all four of us, in Tano's studio makes me feel like we have got to *do* something—and quickly.

"Please, Tano. Can you start looking for a place for us?"

"By myself? After Luzira?" he says. "No way."

Luzira is the name of the neighborhood, and by extension, the house, we lived in when we arrived in Uganda in 1999. I loathed that house with all my being—it was looming, dark, isolated, and I was scared out of my mind every single night—so I badgered and complained and fought with Tano until he agreed to move us into a neighborhood and quarters that I found more livable.

Looking back I can now see the person I was at that time: a young mother burdened by untreated depression and the concurrent notion of having little to no power over what happened to me. (That's the clinical explanation. In Tano's eyes I was just nuts.) It was horrible to be the nag, especially because he was subsumed with the pressures of starting a highly stressful new job. But the hierarchies that I had followed all my life—the job is the boss, the man the second in command, and the women and children have to do what they are told—suddenly didn't matter to me. With a brand new baby in my arms I connected, for the first time, maybe, with the idea that I was not going to just sit back and let everyone else decide for me.

Now, as we take the first steps toward operationalizing our move from Paris to Lyon, I am taxed with all the control that I fought for years to obtain. Still, like a good foot soldier, every evening I search the Internet for places to rent. When I have a list of twelve apartments compiled, I train down to Lyon, Tano takes the day off of work, and we embark on a cyclonic tour of potential new homes.

Of the places we visit, most are either way too big for our family, or filthy and run-down beyond a simple vacuum and paint job. Lyon is a university city—there are thousands of students here—and half of the ads we have responded to neglected to mention that the properties in the soft-light photos have been trashed, year after year, by twenty-year-old slobs. White walls have long since turned yellow from years of nicotine and pot-smoking inhabitants, beautiful old hardwood floors have dulled beneath the grime of a thousand dirty shoes, polishing long abandoned.

"We can't get discouraged," Tano says, and I slip my arm through his, enjoying the sense that we are in this together.

That is, until we visit an apartment I hate even more than the gruesome run-down ones, and Tano says, "Let's take it."

"Take *this*? For our *home?*" We are standing in a modern, frilly wallpapered, highly functional unit with a spacious American-size elevator. It actually feels like a Holiday Inn.

"But it's so…so…*sterile*," I choke.

"Exactly."

"And this neighborhood is so depressing," I whisper, even though the agent showing us the place speaks no English at all.

"*Depressing?* We're ten minutes from the park."

But outside the window all I see are other modern, boxy buildings, and the occasional car. There are no little shops, no restaurants, no historical fountains covered with pigeon poop. The *French* element of this neighborhood is missing. We could be anywhere.

Our last visit is an apartment on place Bellecour. The ad says the apartment has *beaucoup de cachet*—lots of character. I try not to dwell on the fact that the ads for all the other places we visited stated something similar.

But heading to the appointment my spirits start lifting. We are walking through the heart of the Presqu'île, where the distinct charm of the French city abounds: crafted, stylized, majestic. There are the lovely monuments on every other corner that I recognize after the time the kids I spent milling around here. Most importantly, there is *life:* people walking, talking, shopping, sitting in cafés, kissing on benches, standing in line for the movies, at the one, two, no *three* cinemas that we pass....

This is not "anywhere."

This is the France I want to live in.

The weather, which has been cold and gray all day, suddenly lightens, sending agreeable warmth through the parting clouds. All around us people stop to remove coats, hats, scarves. We stop too, peeling off layers, and it occurs to me that a sense of familiarity like this would make leaving Paris for Lyon feel like little more than simply changing *quartier.*

Ten

When we arrive at the address of our last appointment, I can hardly believe it: We are sixty seconds away from Pâtisserie Pignol! If that's not a sign, I don't know what is.

And the building is charming, painted in shades of pink and gray, with tall windows adorned with elegant wrought-iron balconies.

"I love it already," I say.

"Who's the agent?" Tano asks.

I peer at my crumpled list of notes. "A *Monsieur Lamenthe*, I think?"

"Let me see that," he says, reaching for the paper.

I hand it over reluctantly. Tano showed up for our day of apartment hunting with a neat dossier and three sharpened pencils. I showed up with a wad of papers with illegible names scribbled every which way.

"Maybe he's a farmer," I joke, to draw Tano's attention from my messiness by making a little play on words. "Maybe he grows mint for a living."

Tano looks confused.

"*La menthe?*"

"Oh," he says. "Ha. Ha."

My joke really isn't very funny. Also, Mr. Mint Farmer is late.

Tano checks his watch. "We've been waiting for fifteen minutes. Do you have his number?"

The answer, of course, is no, I do not have his number.

At that moment, Monsieur Lamenthe walks up. He is the antithesis of a farmer, rakish in tight jeans, a silk kerchief knotted round his neck, shiny leather lace-ups with long pointy toes. His hair is long in the front and flipped back in a feathered style, the kind of hair that looks like he spent considerable time on it that morning.

"Madame, Monsieur," he says, practically bowing before us. By some impulse of mimicry I, too, do a little curtsy.

"Monsieur Lamenthe?"

"Monsieur *Lamentheur*," he corrects, and Tano shoots me a look. We follow him into the glass-roofed courtyard. The interior stone of the building is cast in gray shadows, lending a haunted quality to this otherwise breathtaking scene: two majestic staircases rise graciously on either side of the courtyard, reminiscent of the secretive stairways of so many castles in the Loire Valley.

As we climb five flights up, Monsieur Lamentheur informs us that the current occupant is a famous Lyonnais interior decorator named Amandine Fontaine. She swings opens the door while Monsieur Lamentheur's finger is still pressed on the bell, and utters only one command: *Entrez.*

Amandine Fontaine is impeccable: stylish and trim, not necessarily beautiful, but not a single molecule out of place. Next to her I feel like a messy spill over.

She declares that she only has fifteen minutes before she has to go back to her boutique on place Bellecour, where some VIP awaits her to discuss his country mansion *relooking*. With that, she leads us into the front hallway, paved in a muted black and white tile, like in a mid-century bourgeois ballroom dance hall. The wall is painted in stripes, whose somber, rich hues are highlighted by the dim lights of fringed chandeliers.

We trot behind Madame Fontaine as she leads us on a tour of the three bedrooms (one of which she uses as her personal closet, with racks and racks of slinky clothes and shelves of high heeled shoes *à la* Carrie Bradshaw).

I glance sideways at Tano when I realize that the plump velour chair in the corner is draped with a silky peignoir and some black garters, dropped on the floor *comme ça*, next to a pair of red-soled Louboutin stilettos. Something tells me these are *not* imitations. I feel a jolt of sex—my mind imagines Amandine Fontaine nude in her garters and heels—and from there a slow motion karma sutra plays out behind my eyelids: Me and Tano in this love pit.

Oh la la.

I float behind Madame Fontaine for the rest of the tour: two bathrooms, a kitchen (painted a deep shade of rose) and a living/dining room that gives onto place Bellecour. The apartment is exactly double the size of our Paris home, big enough to feel the difference, not big enough to get lost in.

Madame Fontaine has decorated exquisitely, with classy velour couches, striking wall hangings, a gorgeous cast iron stove. Although some part of my brain must know that this famous Lyonnais decorator isn't going to just leave the contents of her place with us the way we are bestowing our stylish IKEA furnishings upon our renters, I actually start to feel like I could become an Amandine Fontaine prototype, somehow more perfectly groomed and chic and completely self-contained than I have managed thus far.

I watch as she retrieves a gold lighter and a cigarette from her purse. In one motion she puts the cigarette between her lips, lights, inhales, and releases, her mouth a perfect "O," her expression momentarily languid as the pleasure of a good, deep smoke seeps through her.

Chic.

A la mode.

Très French.

From the fancy furnishings to those stiletto heels that have filled my mind with images of money, and naked, writhing bodies, Amandine Fontaine's entire life, which bears zero resemblance to mine, suddenly appeals to me intensely.

This is the place.

And so why is Tano droning out all these unnecessary questions, like whether Madame Fontaine will be leaving the kitchen and bathrooms intact? I know it's common practice in France to "undress" a rental apartment by removing every last cabinet, counter top, mirror, hook, and light fixture in both the bathroom and the kitchen, not to mention the fridge, stove and oven, but couldn't he focus on what really matters, like how much light is pouring in through the windows, and, as Monsieur Lamentheur cannot stop emphasizing, the charm of the *ancien haute bourgeoisie*?

"Madame," Monsieur Lamentheur says, lowering his voice conspiratorially as he and I look out the living room window. "A place like this is rare. I have a long list of people who want to live here."

"I can imagine," I say. "It is *très charmante…*"

"I assure you, Madame. This is the top area to live in Lyon. I know—I live in the neighborhood myself. You will not regret it. Decide fast, and I'll do everything in my power to give it to *you.*"

Before I can respond, Tano says, to no one in particular, that he is *très concerné* about the amount of work it will take to move into the place. I almost fly across the room to clamp my hand over his mouth.

"Oh, but Monsieur," says Monsieur Lamentheur, "that is but a small detail when you think of the benefit of living at Bellecour." He emphasizes Bellecour with a little sniff of his nose and this tone that says, *Don't you foreigners get it? This is BELLECOUR.*

"It's true!" I jump in, cornering Tano to send him a message with my eyes. *Let's take it!*

But too late: he has gone all serious and says we'll "think" about it.

Think about it?

We part ways, and as soon as Monsieur Lamentheur is out of earshot, I turn to Tano. "*Please Please Please!* This is the *only* apartment that makes sense for our family. I can *see* us in it."

"Can you imagine doing those stairs every single day, several times per day?"

"We're fit. Why not?"

"I'll have to install a kitchen. And a bathroom. By the time Madame-whatever-her-name-is checks out there won't be a single cabinet or surface in the kitchen or bathroom."

"So?"

"Try to visualize this. We will have to shop for *everything*: fridge, stove, cabinets, counters, lights, mirrors for the bathroom…"

"So?"

"And then we'll—no, *I'll*—have to install them."

"But you love doing *bricolage!*"

Bricolage is handiwork, and Tano is a master *bricoleur*, who, in all the years we've been together, has always sought out bricolage projects. His therapy is building and fixing.

I have repressed the details of how I actually manage to convince him (according to Tano the scene involved equal doses of swearing and pleading), but thirty minutes after bidding farewell to Monsieur Lamentheur, Tano calls him to formally submit our dossier.

Given that there are all those other couples beating down the door to rent the place, I'm not sure how our application is approved so quickly.

"Maybe because there aren't any other candidates," Tano offers.

Cynique!

I race back to Paris to tell the kids the exciting news, and we drink a champagne toast with Susan and George. I recount every last detail of our day—all the terrible, horrible places we saw until this last magical one. *The* one. The only detail I leave out is Tano's reluctance. Why dampen the story?

Then we head back upstairs and I call my parents and sisters and Deanna with the details of our wonderful new apartment. I forward everyone the Internet link, and spend countless moments staring at the colorful pictures on the screen as we had once stared at the black and white images in those old Foreign Service post reports.

Everything is falling into place.

Then Tano calls, a few days later, the night before he is to sign the lease. "I have a bad feeling about this," he says. "I don't want to go through with it."

A series of catastrophic thoughts race through my mind: we won't ever find as wonderful a place and we probably won't find *any* place, so we won't have an address, and without an address we can't register the kids for school, and then I'll have to home school them and that is my worst nightmare, and then I will not even be able to come to Paris for work every Monday and Tuesday... *OH GOD!*

"You better sign that contract," I growl.

"Be reasonable, please. If we take that place over by the park..."

"That ugly sterile place?"

"Yes. That ugly, sterile place has a fully equipped kitchen and bathroom. We can move right in and not have to spend a minute on the installation."

"I SWEAR," I shriek. "I will die if I have to live in that horrible apartment. You HAVE to go sign the lease on the other place. The beautiful place."

"It is going to be too much work—"

"PLEASE!"

I won't relay the whole horrible fight. Suffice to say, some hanging up on each other occurs, and I toss and turn for hours that night, visions of my new life as Amandine Fontaine slipping through my grasp. The following morning, I get up and do a series of very mature things, like bombarding Tano with nasty text messages in which I threaten to call the whole move off if he does not rent that fucking apartment.

The singular response I receive to my tirade: "This is great team work."

I know my behavior is abhorrent, that I am acting like a petulant child. But deep down I feel that he owes me this apartment, and a veritable psychological phenomenon is interfering with my ability to take *no* for an answer. The last time I crossed the threshold of our new home was ten years ago, and I was alone with my toddler in a complete crisis. Those visions of our last move are conjoined with memories of the collapse of our marriage. Coupled with the fact that the stable home I forged for myself and our kids is now being dismantled, I feel really quite desperate. I *have* to be in control of what happens this time. I can't help it: I link brick and mortar stability with psychological stability; that interplay between geography and personal crisis is forever present in my mind.

But by afternoon Tano's silence works to significantly reduce my hysteria, and I am already feeling compunctious. By evening all I can think about is a story my big sister Lesley told me, of when she had some similar type of fit when her husband didn't want to buy a dining room table she'd spotted at an estate sale. She made such a fuss all the way home and just couldn't let it go, that he finally left the house. An hour later he reappeared, with the table and its twelve chairs. She felt horrible for the way she'd carried on—the guilt of getting your own way, she called it—and that feeling only compounded when she discovered that the table (and its twelve chairs) really *was* too big for their house.

By the time I go to bed that night, the verdict is in: Tano signed the lease. But contrition over my tantrum all but destroys any fresh excitement at this news. "Thank you," I whisper.

All he answers, in that voice whose quiet tenor is enough to make me feel like the biggest brat on earth: "Installing a kitchen, a bathroom, getting the materials up all those stairs…It's going to be a lot of work."

I try to console him with the only thing I am certain about: It isn't like the bum dining room table. It's going to be wonderful.

It has to be.

Eleven

Every time my family moved with the Foreign Service, logistical front men of the US government would arrive at our house a few weeks before our departure, truckloads of boxes and packing tape in tow. Under my parents' supervision, they would move through the house with amazing speed, packing everything for us, loading a portion of "essentials" into the overnight air freight and the "less essentials" into a slower sea freight. Some other logistics manager would see to it that we were lodged in a hotel and fed in restaurants until we had a stable place, in the new country, to live again.

Every relocation I have done with Tano has been far less complicated—materially speaking, that is. As there was never a budget to move with, we did not cross borders with much *stuff*.

From New Orleans to Nairobi we moved with a suitcase each.

Two years later, when we shifted from Nairobi to Kampala, that allotment had expanded to several boxes, because we had some paraphernalia to accommodate the only "thing" of any real importance we were transporting: our newborn baby.

When I flew screaming out of Uganda two years later, that baby, by then a toddler, was in one arm, a single duffel bag for the two of us in the other.

One weekend shortly before our departure, Tano stays in Lyon to move his belongings from his studio to our wonderful new apartment, and I devote myself to sorting through the material trappings of our Parisian life. Though we have been constrained to 635 square feet, we have had a solid ten years in Paris to accrue things. So even though we are leaving all of our furniture behind, I fill bag after bag with those relics of my children's lives that are un-leavable: Carmen's prized *papier maché* dog, Lorenzo's ping pong ball eyeballs, the lopsided ceramic ashtrays they made down on the first floor with Matthew (in spite of George's gentle reminder that neither Tano nor I smoke).

Then there are the boxes that bulge with their most beloved toys—a perfume-making kit, three naked Action men, sets of Hot Wheels cars…

There are all of my books, photo albums, our music collection… and then I find it, the folder of our most private past that I knew, of course, was *somewhere*, and yet I was not quite ready to find again. I can't bear to look through it, but I also can't bear not to.

I open the cover tentatively. On top is the thick stack of e-mails from Tano, sent in the months after I left him. He is heartbroken, he writes. He threw away the best thing he ever had by getting involved with "that" woman; and for nothing, because there was absolutely nothing between them. It was "just" sex.

There are as many e-mails from me, messages typed in all caps, an attempt to scream my sarcastic rage through the Ethernet cables.

"JUST" SEX?

"THAT" WOMAN?
IS THAT MEANT TO CONSOLE ME?

In a strange twist, the fact that Tano dropped his lover's name—Estelle—in favor of referring to her as "that woman," increased my fury. Did he think he was Bill Clinton, and that he could deflect responsibility from his actions by depersonalizing her? And even if he had had the grace to call her by her name, given that we barely touched each other anymore by the time I learned of the affair, the "just sex" justification only filled me with more jealousy and rejection.

But I also didn't believe the "just sex" argument, not for one second. I know men and women are ostensibly different this way, but I did not see how it was possible to have been sleeping with and sharing meals with and working and traveling with "that" woman and not develop feelings. I suspected they loved each other. Tano was not stupid: why the hell would he risk his family for someone he didn't even care for?

Compounding this disbelief was the fact that Estelle was not by any appearances a sexpot, the kind of woman you imagine your husband would fall for. At least not if it was for "just sex."

Until that moment, I had spent much of (my entire?) life believing that my greatest source of power came from being provocative and alluring. The popular princess-and-the-pea type fairy tales of my childhood taught me that; as did growing up with cultural icons like Madonna. From adolescence and well into my adulthood I worked very hard at my sexual image. Even at the height of our marital crisis, when Tano and I no longer seemed to be able to stand each other, I still believed that if I could just seduce him everything would turn out alright.

Oh, there were plenty of signs along the way that this was a misguided notion. One particularly awful squabble in Nairobi stands out. Tano went to Sudan for two weeks, and though he had a satellite phone with him, he did not call me, not even once.

"I can't run up the MSF phone bill just to say hello!" he'd insisted when I lit into him upon his return, an awful mixture of relief that he was alright and betrayal that he hadn't cared to maintain contact with me fueling my fury. His parsimonious explanation did not assuage my anger because I already knew, from multiple conversations with other MSF wives, that the other staff did not feel nearly as concerned about MSF's phone bill and used the available technology to keep in touch when they went to far-flung, dangerous locations.

As these things went, my anger made him withdraw and he walked away from me and closed the door to his office. I panicked. He was going to be leaving again the next day and I could not bear to think that we'd part on bad terms. So I whipped off my clothes and put on some outrageously sexy little lace thing that I had acquired along the way and then planted myself on his lap while he tried to do some data entry in preparation for his impending departure.

"This will not work on me," he said, his lips in a grim line. "I am mad at you and I cannot just have sex on command."

The nerve of him! I remember thinking. I stewed in the bedroom and then he appeared, suddenly. *Ha! It worked!*

But then I lost Tano, at least for a time, to someone who didn't pay attention at all to her appearance. Amorphous

T-shirts, no makeup, short, choppy hair that she clearly had been cutting herself. Oh what a confusing and painful revelation it was. The prettier girl *didn't* win, and clearly, the affair was not about "just" sex.

My heart clenches up at the memory of my skewed sense of self, and I literally ache for that wounded creature. At the ripe age of 40 I could remember who I was at 30: a fragile young woman who actually believed in sexual provocativeness as a form of insurance, who learned in a horrible way that it was a completely false security.

I put down the folder and go to the mirror, leaning up close to look into my own eyes. My breath forms a cloud on the glass. *You've come a long way, Baby*, I think, remembering how, after our break up, bit by bit I relinquished many of the ways I formerly attempted to be enticing. I stopped making eye contact with men I didn't know, stopped smiling coyly at strangers, stopped wearing such revealing clothes. Instead I slowly weaned myself into comfortable pants and shoes, simple T-shirts, nothing flashy or revealing. And the less visible I became sexually, the better I felt about myself intellectually. I realize now, with hindsight, what a radical act of self-protection it was to walk away from the game of sexual titillation.

The phone rings. It is Susan. "Want to pop down for a drink?"

Ten minutes later I am sprawled out on Susan and George's couch, enjoying a glass of wine and periodically breaking into coughing fits, the day's packing having generated so much dust that particles of my family's history are now permanently embedded in my lungs.

Susan and George have agreed to keep this folder of loaded emotional history for me. I cannot bear to throw these traces of the past away any more than I can bear to carry them into my new life in Lyon. We have just finished storing the dossier in the back of a high shelf when Tano calls. I snatch up the phone and in one long, uninterruptible sentence tell him how I worked all day and it was super productive and I've got the bags organized and now Susan and George are feeding me and...Tano? Are you there?

"There are 98 steps." His voice is ever so quiet, but boy, does he sound pissed.

"What?"

"From the front entrance on rue du Président Edouard Herriot to our door on the fifth floor, there are *98 steps*. I had to make twenty trips up and down those stairs today."

My thighs throb just thinking about it.

I beckon to George for more wine, and by the time my glass has been filled, Tano and I have gotten off the phone.

"Oh, God," I say, pressing on my temples.

"What?" Susan says. "What happened?"

"The new apartment. The stairs. It was a hard day." I gulp my wine. "It's all my fault."

"That's crazy—of course it's not your fault. He agreed to live there. It's not like it was something you pressured him into."

I shoot her a guilty look and she squints her eyes. "Is there something you haven't told us?" She doesn't wait for the answer. "George! Bring another bottle."

While Susan and George listen, wide-eyed, I recount my bullish temper tantrum of a few weeks back, and they gasp at the right moments and finally laugh at my utter gall. And just as I am comforted, as always, by their presence in my life, I am again struck by the panic of losing this connection when I leave.

And then, before I can even blink twice, it is the end of June and I am closing my office for the summer. I won't be back until the second week of September—eleven full weeks away. I have not taken this much time off of work since Lorenzo was born, and the prospect is exciting. Eleven weeks in Lyon to get the kids settled, the apartment set up, to reconnect with Tano—hell, to reconnect with *myself*—in this new chapter of our life.

As I turn my key in the lock for the very last time until September, Deanna pokes her head out of her office window. "This is it, huh?"

"The beginning of the end."

She shoots me a look. I know I am being negative.

"Okay, okay," I say. "The beginning of the new chapter."

We stare at each other for a long moment. She has lost all her hair but decided against getting a wig when she discovered that her bald head has a gorgeous oval shape. The clinic where she is receiving treatment has a beauty salon and she has been experimenting with makeup and big hoop earrings. Amazingly, she feels pretty good in spite of the chemo—only tired—and she looks beautiful, her eyes luminous and her smile more radiant than ever, without her hair to compete for attention.

"Can I come up and say good-bye?"

"I'll come down," she says. "I'm on my way out. I have a chemo appointment."

She comes down the stairs and we stand silently for a moment before the closed door of my office, once our shared domain. I remember intensely what it was like to find the space, to set it up, and I feel this regressive longing for that wonderful time we shared.

We hug. "Keep me posted, girlfriend," I say.

"I will," she promises. "I will."

LYON 2011

Twelve

Exactly twenty-four hours later Tano meets me, the kids, and our heap of bags at Gare Part-Dieu in Lyon, and we taxi to the new apartment. It *is* somehow exciting to pile out of the taxi onto the sidewalk of our new place, but once inside the courtyard, we are faced with the stairs. There is no way I am going to let Tano carry all this crap up for me, not after everything he's already been through.

But those stairs, those 98 stairs…They tower straight into the sky, seeming very, very, *very* tall when contemplating the task of hauling up all this gear I decided was "essential" to our well-being.

I eye the garbage bins.

But without saying anything vindictive, like, "Now *you* carry up all the bags, so you can see what it feels like," my lovely, chivalrous man refuses to let me go it alone. He loads as much as he can onto his back and begins the hike up, which he is now somehow used to, (unlike me, who is sweating by the thirtieth step).

Inside the apartment the children run through the rooms. *I can't believe how big it is!* they shout. *This is great, Mom!*

And although I cheerily agree with them, privately another thought is coming to me: *Tano was right.* I can't believe how much work we're going to have to do to make this place liveable.

Because the apartment *is* naked.

"Oh my God," I gasp, noting the twisted wires dangling barbarically from the high ceilings where Madame Fontaine's fancy chandeliers once hung. "She really did take everything."

"Yup," Tano says, his mouth in a grim line. "She didn't leave us a single lightbulb. She even took the *sockets*."

The things that Tano had accumulated over eighteen months in his single-during-the-week life are strewn about, creating the impression that the apartment has been squatted by a bag lady. A couple of small table lamps sit in a row in the marble hallway, next to four pocket flashlights. He sees me glance at them and says, "I just bought them. For when it gets dark out."

Without Madame Fontaine's fancy furnishings, I can see now how much dirt is actually caked into the dark crevices once covered by rugs; the worn and torn aspect of the walls once covered by paintings. *Fusty* is the word that comes to mind.

I sigh. "It's such a mess."

"That's because there's not a single surface to put things on," he snaps. "No shelves, no counters, nothing."

I hadn't intended to sound critical, and certainly not of Tano, but with the reality of our situation seeping into my consciousness, I can't quite muster the energy to explain. Instead, I duck into the bathroom so that I can see for myself something he'd already told me over the phone—that there's no longer any mirror—but with no windows and no lightbulbs it's too dark to even verify that. I go in search of the flashlight.

Tano has already acquired a refrigerator for us, and in a fit of angst the night before in Paris, I did a huge online grocery order. Now, standing amidst this mayhem, it arrives. I watch, embarrassed, as though the five flights are my own moral failing, while the young, muscular deliveryman struggles up the 98 stairs under the weight of all our food products. In fact, he is panting so heavily I fear he is going to have a heart attack, although in time I will learn that even the fittest souls are gasping by the time they arrive at our door.

So we add the ton of groceries to the chaos and then establish that we need to go out for dinner anyway because there was a delivery glitch and the new stove will not arrive until tomorrow.

"Okay, kids," I rally. "Shoes on. We're heading back down the mountain."

Thirteen

Lyon is considered the gastronomic capital of France.

In fact, since I began announcing our move to Lyon, there has been a standard response from the Parisian crowd. It begins with a sharp puff of air from between pursed lips, followed by, *C'est pas Paris*—It's not Paris.

This commiseration is consistently followed by: *"Au moins vous allez manger bien."*

At least you'll eat well.

There are more than 1,500 restaurants in Lyon, a healthy handful of them with Michelin stars. This famed rating system is an endorsement of dining quality, as in fine dining, which I once found hilarious, given that Michelin is a tire manufacturer. And their logo looks like a man dressed in a suit of marshmallows. But you can't live for an extended period in France without learning that the *Michelin Guide* actually started as a reference for motorists on places to eat outside of Paris, and the marshmallow man, named Bibendum, not only got his name from one of Horace's classical works, but is also one of the oldest trademarks in the world.

One of France's most celebrated chefs, Paul Bocuse, hails from Lyon, where, in addition to several Michelin-starred restaurants, he set up Les Halles, an acclaimed indoor market brimming with meats, seafood, cheeses, wines and desserts—only the best, most refined products.

Lyon is perhaps most known, though, for its *bouchons*, famed not for *haute cuisine* but for providing a casual, even jovial atmosphere in which to eat hearty, traditional dishes, such as blood sausages, cow's stomach, or brain pâté. I had assumed that restaurants as such were called bouchon—a word that means plug or cork but that also translates as "traffic jam"—because the food immediately clogs one's arteries. But as it turns out, the name actually came about because the owners of these eateries, as far back as the 1600s, had the tradition of tying little bundles of branches, known as "*bousche*" in the old Lyonnais dialect, on the door to let customers know they were open. Over time, the word evolved into the French bouchon.

A lovely story, indeed, but we don't go out in search of a bouchon that first evening in Lyon, for while the menu in these establishments might excite, say, an Argentinean carnivore, it is far less appealing to those of us who keep a mostly vegetarian diet.

Out on the sidewalk in front of our new place it takes a moment to get oriented. Without the throngs of shoppers milling about I am now able to take closer note of the "shops" on our street: Hermès, Cartier, Louis Vuitton, Furla, MaxMara, Swarovski…

I have booked us into the Lyonnais equivalent of Paris's rue Saint Honoré. Beverly Hills's Rodeo Drive. New York's 5th Avenue.

Now, if I haven't made it clear enough why this might cause some unease, let me repeat: we are simple people ourselves.

"Dressing up" means wearing black jeans instead of blue, city sneakers instead of flip flops. My beloved Quartier Oberkampf feels suddenly very far away and my notion of becoming some sort of Amandine Fontaine clone utterly ridiculous. What on earth was I thinking?

We find a stretch of restaurants on rue des Marronniers, many of which clearly cater to the tourist crowd. The menus are in English, offering some very funny translations of eating fatty lard in sauce. I am tired and overwhelmed, but it is impossible to sink into grouchiness, not with the animated chatter of the wait staff, all of whom want to practice their English, and all of whom offer forth lavish praise to me for being… *American?*

J'adore votre petit accent! they say. *J'adore les Etats-Unis!*

In all the years I've interfaced with the French until now, I have basically stuffed any active sense of patriotism or cultural pride into the deep recesses of my mind. Life with an openly anti-American francophone team during the years in East Africa with MSF, as well as a certain scornful attitude of many Parisians toward English speakers, has never encouraged me to speak openly about any reasons I might be *proud* of being American. (The one exception being the glorious victory of Barack Obama in 2008. When he was elected, *everyone* in Paris—French, American, even Japanese tourists—shook hands and embraced me in the street.)

This is not to say that I ever accepted the anti-American jokes, snarky comments, or imitations of my accent when I speak French. But these are not things I ever defended myself against with any ease. Rather, I tended to avoid anyone who I knew to be rude, and even boycotted my preferred neighborhood grocery store in Paris because of being mocked by two particularly odious cashiers.

In Lyon the pendulum seems to have swung the other way, and I am instantly esteemed for where I am from.

It is a strange thing, this cultural identity stuff. The waiter babbles on about the trips he has made to New York and Los Angeles—*j'adoooooore!*—but in a mind shift, I'm back at a court-yard *apéro* at the Oberkampf kibbutz one spring evening several years ago.

The three oldest kids of the building—Carmen, Matthew, and Zoë, ages 10, 9, and 8 at the time—have formed a *"Club des Meilleurs"* (Club of the Best) and pooled their money to buy some Nintendo games. I am chatting with the biggest gaming junkie of the building, a thirty-something man named Christophe.

Carmen runs up to us, face flushed with excitement. "We have 31 euros! Christophe, how much did you have to spend to get all your games?"

Christophe studies my daughter for a long second and then answers, with what sounds like disapproval, *"We* don't talk about money. Not in France."

"Okay," Carmen accepts, blithely skipping off back to her friends.

But my face burns. Are we that culturally out of balance?

That brief exchange speaks to that *thing* that seems to come and go, without warning, in our daily lives here in France, in particular for the kids who blend in neatly, the quintessential hidden immigrants, who can "pass" as local until their foreign parents give them away. I bumble along thinking we're assimilated and then something will happen, some wrong thing said, or some thing said wrong, and suddenly we are back in a "you versus us" dialogue.

Not that this is any different from the way cultural differences play out elsewhere. In all the countries I lived in growing up, my very appearance revealed that I was a foreigner. My sensibility about my own kids' sense of assimilation in France has to do with my desire for them to feel that they truly belong. Because unlike my childhood, where there was never a doubt that I would ultimately leave the countries I lived in, my kids do not live with the shadow of repatriation lurking near. Ostensibly we are here to stay, and this is their "real" life.

The *pop!* of the cork of the bottle we've ordered breaks the connection to the past. The garrulous waiter retreats, and Carmen says, "God, Mom, that guy really likes you."

"It's not that he really likes *me*, personally. But I guess he thinks it's cool to be American."

Carmen looks pleased with this information. "Why?"

"Well, a lot of people associate certain things that they really like with American culture."

"Like Michael Jackson?" Lorenzo pipes up.

"Yes," I say, "But it's also about attitudes. Like being positive and optimistic. Many French people have told me they see those qualities as being very American."

"Like 'Yes We Can'?" Carmen asks.

"Yep."

"Like Barack Obama?" Lorenzo adds, clearly pleased to have made the connection.

"Exactly. You see, Americans have a reputation for believing that if you work hard, you can make whatever you dream of come true."

"Is that true?" Carmen asks. "That if you work hard enough you can make your dreams come true?"

I think about it for a moment, and decide to go with "Yes." Of course, dreams coming true involves more than hard work, but this is clearly a moment of cultural indoctrination.

"But Mom?" Carmen says. "How do we ever know if something good or bad about us is because of who we are and not because of where we're from?"

My children's questions about identity so often emerge in ways I don't expect, and without fail, force me to consider this very matter.

As she banged noisily on her father's guitar at age eight, I finally shouted, "Knock it off, Carmen! You're driving me crazy!"

"But Mom," she answered, "I only feel Argentinean when I play the guitar."

Without the tinny, raucous strumming to rattle my nerves, I might never have known that "feeling Argentinean"—identifying with her father, and his faraway family—was, at some deeper level, of concern to her.

So I changed my tune. "Keep playing, darling. You're getting there."

A year or so later she emerged from her dance class one hot spring afternoon with an expression of preoccupied gloom. "Look at my face, Mom," she whispered, tears spilling over. "The other girls say that it gets all red because I'm American."

I assured her that citizenship had nothing to do with whose face gets red, and reminded her of all the red-faced people we know who are as French as they come. But something was brewing inside her—I could sense it—and it came out a few nights later when she broke down crying. "No one understands me. I can't manage to do things exactly the way a true French person does."

Yet she was saying this to her American mom, who marveled at her daughter's beautiful little French accent, the way she held her fork, the curlicues of her so very French handwriting, the way she tied little scarves *just so* around her neck. By then she had been immersed in French culture for seven years. She had done all of her schooling in Paris. I often wondered how I ended up with a French child.

I bumbled through some commentary that was meant to be reassuring: Surely the other kids understood her. She wasn't *that* different.

But she only cried harder. "You don't understand me either, Mom. I'm not French the way they are, and I'm not American the way you are. I just don't belong anywhere."

Tonight, in Lyon, I still don't have a definitive answer to that question of what, first and foremost, makes us who we are, and so I say what I have always said: It's case by case. Some things are by nature, some things are by culture, and usually, the two things end up influencing each other, anyway.

Fourteen

Home from dinner, we plug in the table lamps in strategic corners, distribute the flashlights, and then I walk from room to room, counting the windows of our new Lyonnais apartment. The Oberkampf nest has a total of four windows; this one has eleven. Many of them are floor to ceiling with a little standing balcony. Now I go to the one in the room we have designated as Lorenzo's and step out into the evening air. Something about the hanging gray of the night sky and the warm breeze reminds me of so many other moments, at once completely familiar yet totally un-pinpoint-able: it is the feeling of arriving somewhere tropical. I raise my face to the moon, effervescent and full, hanging low over place Bellecour, and say a little prayer: *Please God, give me a sign that we're all going to be okay.*

This is, in fact, a little prayer from my childhood, first concocted in response to the horrible sounds of my sisters, who had both caught the latest school stomach flu, throwing up one night when we were all little and still lived in Washington, DC. The same prayer saw me through multiple episodes of childhood anxiety, most of which circled around fear of plane crashes and terminal illness, ideas inherited from various news sources and transposed to the unknowns of my young life: long journeys to new countries, new schools, new cultures.

Then Lorenzo appears and tugs at my arm. "Can we go home now, Mom?"

Oh, God. A six year old in denial.

"This *is* our new home, sweetheart. We're going to sleep here tonight."

"And then we go back at Paris?"

"We're not going back *to* Paris, honey. This is our new home, and we're going to live here, and tomorrow when we're not so tired we'll try to straighten up this mess and buy some furniture."

He seems to be weighing this answer, but he is also yawning with a wide, open mouth. The day has been utterly exhausting. Only Carmen and Tano are still buzzing around with their flashlights, Carmen in the excited throes of interior decoration fantasy, and her devoted bricoleur father, who in spite of his upset about the apartment I have condemned him to, with a proactive attitude about the different projects he'll undertake to fix it up.

I help Lorenzo get ready for bed while Tano sets up the air mattress, and then we tuck him in together. The first night in his new room, the first time in his six-year-old life that he's ever had his *own* room.

He lasts about one minute.

"Mom!"

I run to him. He is sitting up in bed, his flashlight casting shadows on the empty walls.

"I'm *scared*, Mom. This place is way too big."

I hold him close. "You're going to be okay, darling. It's going to be okay."

I persuade Carmen to get ready for bed so that I can tuck Lorenzo in next to her. Although at first she expresses irritation—her first night in *her* very own room upended by her little brother—deep down I think she appreciates his proximity. She isn't scared herself, but it is less lonely to go to sleep together. She has been sharing a room with him, after all, for the last six years.

Then, thank God, it is finally time for us to go to bed, as well. I debate a quick shower —my armpits are not going to win any perfume awards this evening—but I am too wiped out to bother. I stretch out on our squishy blow-up mattress.

The sensation of the mattress squashing in toward the middle pulls me back from near sleep. Every move Tano makes causes the entire bed to dip and pucker. And *whoa*—he also could use some help in the armpit department.

Oblivious, he pulls me toward him. "I'm so glad you're here with me now."

I allow myself to be drawn into him, but I am distracted, trying to keep my arms pressed to my sides. My mind goes to OCD mode, chanting *stairs furniture grime, stairs furniture grime,* and then finally hovers around this image of Lorenzo, that sad confusion in his face, his question: Why can't we go back "at" Paris? Why can't we go home?

I bury my face in Tano's neck and try to focus on the reason I am here. But behind my eyelids all I see is myself, dishing out advice to the Parents' Group in Paris: *It's so much easier to move a young child than a teenager.* I give in to the futility of keeping our armpits to ourselves and think what had I really known about any of this?

Fifteen

I n the weeks that follow I have to face other disturbing truths about how insufficient my own advice is. For example, I cannot recall ever giving any talks about the fact that moving can be so stressful that you may suddenly realize that you hate your spouse—at least for small, vitriolic moments—for putting you in the situation. Because while he is at work, you are stuck at home with the boxes and the bickering children. Although maybe none of those women I lectured had ever done something as stupid as I have: yanking the kids out of their community so that they can spend a long summer in a new place with *nothing* to do.

Except torment each other and cling to Mommy.

Because *that* is the situation: The kids and I are glued to each other, 24–7, for the whole, long summer. Visions of my sensual new Lyonnais life disappear into thin air.

Reality check: the kids have no friends to meet up with, and I have a household to organize. And if for one moment it sounds fun to furnish an *entire household* from scratch, let me tell you, dear Reader, it isn't, not with a depressed, oppositional six year old in tow, and an exuberant twelve year old whose desire to *spend spend spend* does not match up with her parents' more impecunious habits. Not to mention the stress of having to lug every piece of furniture we buy up the 98 stairs (Yes, delivery service exists in France, but Mr. DIY would as soon commit hara-kiri than pay someone to do the backbreaking work that we can do ourselves).

The whole ordeal is like being on a reality TV challenge show, where our family is put under extreme stress to see how we fare.

Challenge number 1: The IKEA packages. They arrive by the ton while Tano is at work, so heavy that Carmen and I are obligated to open boxes at the bottom of the stairs and haul entire furniture sets up, plank by plank.

Challenge number 2: The beds. The mattresses arrive vacuum packed into tight cylindrical sausages with the dismantled (extremely heavy) bed frames. We leave Lorenzo at the bottom of the stairs to guard the heap of stuff, lest any vulturine passersby think it's a pile of giveaways. When we come panting back down the stairs we are shocked to see that he has single-handedly cut into the binding plastic wrap and the mattresses have sprung out of their casing, while he looks on in wonder.

Challenge number 3: The desk. Our torturous installation comes to a head the Saturday we buy the oak desk, which looks so pretty in the store and is on sale at half price because it is the *modèle d'exposition*—the shop model. The burly vendors load it on to a caddy, which they loan us for exactly one hour—any longer we'll have to pay—the time it should take for us to wheel it down the street to our apartment.

Easy.

But when we unload the desk at the bottom of our stairs, we are shocked by its weight. It is *so fucking heavy.*

"How the hell are we going to carry this up the stairs?" I ask Tano, already visualizing one of us crushed by the desk, our legs twitching grotesquely from underneath it.

"We'll manage," Tano says, ever the optimist. As usual, he takes the heaviest side, but my "light" side is still so heavy I have to enlist Carmen to help. Lorenzo is unhappy that he is the only one without a job, so he darts up and down the stairway, augmenting the tension, for if the desk slips from our grasps and crashes down the stairs, anyone in its path will be a goner.

"Get *up* the stairs," I shriek, repeatedly, "*UP!*" Soon Carmen and Tano are also screeching at him, Carmen in French, Tano in Spanish. Neighbors in the building open their windows to see what sort of polyglotinous psychodrama is playing out: Do we even *know* that kid that we can't decide what language to speak to?

By the time we get the desk to the top of the stairs, we are all in a sweat, and Lorenzo is in tears. I comfort and reprimand him all at once and am stunned when Tano tells me how pissed off he is at *me*.

"What did *I* do?" I snap.

"You were unreasonable." His eyes flick to the front door of the apartment and he need say no more. I know now that he was right. In fact, I privately took his side of the argument about five minutes after we arrived the first night. I chose the wrong apartment for us. I did not work as a team with Tano, I just charged ahead with my own bull-headed vision, muddled by my angst about moving, some fuzzy idea about making up for past regrets, and a ridiculous notion of a fancy new me.

And now we are stuck.

I feel like a total jerk.

Yet the situation will later strike me as a portent. Hauling that desk five flights up, and the different ways it affects each one of us, is the perfect metaphor for all that is hard about not just this move, but this existence, from the literal (we have no one around to help us, no family, no intimate friends), to the symbolic (the weight of that desk is like the weight of the world, trying to assemble a life when nothing is familiar and it's all uphill).

A few days later, the phone rings. It is the *livreurs*, calling to set up the delivery of the new dining room table. They will be pulling up in front of our building at exactly 2:30 that afternoon, and I need to be there to supervise the drop off.

Drop off?

It is a solid mahogany table we have ordered. There is no way Carmen and I will ever be able to get it up the stairs, and we can't leave it down on the sidewalk all day.

In an act of desperation-driven spontaneity, I quaver, "This is how you treat a handicapped woman?"

"Vous êtes handicappée, Madame?"

The brusque tone changes entirely: They sound genuinely concerned. I hesitate for a split second. Dare I lie about something so serious? Then an image of those stairs flashes before my eyes.

"Oui," I say, managing a perfect pitch to convey bravery in the face of dire straits. *"Je suis handicappée."*

And that settles it.

Sixteen

Tano is shocked to see the massive table in the center of the dining room when he gets home that evening. "How on earth did you get it up the stairs?"

I let him in on my little trick and he gapes with such stupefaction that I brace myself for a lecture. But all he says is: "Don't you think it's a little suspect that a handicapped woman would live five flights up with no elevator?"

Good point.

"If you're going to lie, at least say something realistic. Like you have cancer, for example."

"Are you crazy?" My stomach knots up at his words. Back in Paris, Deanna is days away from having a mastectomy. Though I am pleasantly surprised that my upstanding husband will play along with my subterfuge, I cannot believe he would suggest *cancer* as the thing I should fake.

Is it anxiety about Deanna's surgery, or the tension of the last few weeks, or simply guilt that from my ivory tower I tricked some poor delivery guys into hauling that stupid table five flights up? Because suddenly I am too exhausted to even talk. Without a word I float to the bedroom and lie face down on the mattress.

"Are you alright?" Tano asks, crouching by the bedside. "What happened?"

But so much has happened, and is *still* happening; I don't think I can explain it. Suffice to say: I cannot believe I was ever considered a "specialist" on helping families move, let alone helping other trailing spouses resolve their difficulties as I personally am about to go mental.

The kids come in search of me. "Mom?" I pull a pillow over my head. "Mooooom! I'm hungry!"

When they find me on the bed, Tano sitting next to me with God-knows-what expression on his face, they become concerned. Lorenzo hugs my legs and Carmen tries to pull the pillow off my head. "Mom?"

The tone in her voice is so totally apprehensive that it tasers me back to calm. Clearly she counts on seeing me as the invincible, in charge, energetic person that she believes me to be. And an invincible, in charge, energetic Mom does not crawl into bed at dinnertime unless something is seriously wrong.

I take a deep breath and sit up. "I'm fine," I say. "But I need a break from this furnishing-the-apartment business."

And with that I declare a moratorium on the seemingly interminable task of furniture shopping. What I want to do is pull the covers over my head for several months, but the kids still have their eyes on their fearless leader. And so, declaring that we *are* going to have a wonderful time whether we like it or not, I drag the kids around Lyon.

We visit: the Centre d'Histoire de la Résistance et de la Déportation, a museum with detailed expositions on the French resistance during World War II, where Lorenzo falls down the stairs and screams so loudly the staff beg me to allow them to call an ambulance; the Musée des Frères Lumières, which commemorates the Lyonnais brothers who invented the *cinematographe*, where I fall asleep in the cool, dark *salle de film* and, to the kids' horror, snore; and the Musée des Beaux Arts, which we charge through in thirty seconds, missing the Egyptian collection and the portrait gallery (with its assortment of Rubens, Gauguins, Picassos, Manets, Monet, and Matisses, to name just a few), on our way to the real point of the visit: the idyllic courtyard restaurant.

There we snarf down a *flan aux crèmes des marrons*, a *fondant au chocolat*, and the lightest, airiest *Ile Flotante* I have ever had the pleasure of eating.

Over these gorgeous desserts, Lorenzo says, "Why can't we go back at Paris, Mom?" His voice sounds so wholly forlorn he might well be a refugee asking why the rebels burned down his village.

"We can't go back *to* Paris, my love," I say, "because in life we sometimes have to make changes. This is one of those times." My answer is undoubtedly unsatisfying, but he already knows the other spiel: *Pop's new job, sticking together as a family, blah blah blah.*

"Well, I hate Lyon," he says, "and I hate *you* for making us come here."

I am tempted to say, "You think this was my idea?" but then he says, "I wish I didn't exist."

Rationally, I know that what sounds like a statement of profound existential crisis is probably just raw homesickness presented in the peculiar mixed vocabulary of a bilingual six year old. But it sounds alarmingly bleak and for a split second his grief transports me back in time to all the unresolved loss of my own childhood.

I ask Carmen and Lorenzo if they'd like to hear some stories of times *I* had to move when I was a kid.

Yes!

So I tell them how when I was nine, and we left DC for the Ivory Coast, I felt so anxious about taking the long flight that I swiped Rolaids from my parents' bathroom cabinet, convinced that they held some magic property that would prevent anything bad from happening (and then I explain, in terms that both kids can understand, what an anxiety disorder is, lest they think this is an adaptive way of coping).

How the night we left the Ivory Coast four years later, I cried and cried and our houseboy Celestin clasped my hands and said, "*Pourquoi tu pleures comme ça quand tu n'as que treize ans?*" Why are you crying like this when you're only thirteen? (Because I was sad, and it's okay to express sadness. It helps, even.)

How when I was fifteen and my family was leaving Cairo for good, the Embassy put us up in a hotel for our last night, and a group of friends came to the room I shared with Lesley. We were all distressed and broke into a group sob fest that escalated into so much howling that the manager of the hotel tried to evict us in the middle of the night. (My father was not pleased, but it really *is* okay to express sadness, although it's not okay to be inconsiderate of other people.)

How two years later on the last night of our tour in New Delhi, I turned my back on an old, dear friend to spend time with someone I had known just a few weeks and thought I was in love with. (There is a poem that illustrates what I learned that night: *Make new friends, but keep the old…*)

How when I left Indonesia for the very last time, our house-keeper, Suki, whom we had been close to for four years, had mis-understood when I was leaving and wasn't back from the market in time to see me off. My mother sent me a letter saying how Suki had cried when she learned that we had missed each other for that very final good-bye.

I cried, too.

Lorenzo finds these stories extremely interesting, and that night as I tuck him in next to Carmen he has questions: Why didn't I just go back to those places for a visit? (Too many places, too far away, not enough time or money.)

Did I send Suki a letter? (I did.)

Was my Dad still mad about the crying fit in Cairo? (He wasn't.)

Were the Rolaids magic? (Yes, if you believe in placebos.)

"Should you really be filling his head with all these dramatics?" Tano asks, standing in the doorway and listening, as riveted, it seems, as our son. I stick my tongue out at him and continue, for what he doesn't know is that I am trying to model something therapeutic for Lorenzo. This *is*, in fact, the very essence of tra-ditional therapy, at least as I understand it: narrating the saga, explaining, making sense of stories. If I can model that for my son, perhaps he will be better able to do it for himself. I want to show him that people are resilient. I was; he will be, too.

But his homesickness is as glaring as the midday Lyonnais sun (Fact: the sun actually shines brighter in Lyon than in Paris) and as loud as the rabblerousers that party down on place Bellecour every night. His yearning to go home floods into my veins, as though we are still attached by the umbilical cord. All the repressed loss—people and places of my life that are forever gone—comes back to me now. I understand Lorenzo's longing more than he can know, and this symbiotic suffering makes me that much more grateful that our little apartment in Paris is still there for us. Its existence, and the fact that we can go back, provides the very symbol of continuity that was missing in my own childhood.

"I wish I had a magic wand," Lorenzo says as I kiss him goodnight. "I'd wave it and we'd go back at Paris forever."

"Well if I had a magic wand," Carmen says, "I would wave it at you and make you happy again."

"I'll never never never be happy again," he counters.

I close the door gently, leaving them to argue over whether there is any chance at happiness ever again in this cruel world. In the hallway I find Tano peering through the peephole in the front door.

"What are you—?"

"Shhhhhh! Listen!"

I freeze in my tracks. Through the door I hear the raspy, wheezy sound of…heavy breathing? The sound intensifies and then Tano steps back, shrugging. "I hope there's a defibrillator in this building."

He goes down the hallway and I take his place at the peephole. Outside on the landing is an old woman with long dark hair, her face wrinkled up like a walnut. She is visibly hunchbacked yet has a parcel thrown over her shoulders that she seems to be collapsing under. She clutches the banister with one hand and gasps for breath. *Pant pant pant...*

Suddenly she pulls a pack of cigarettes from her pocket and lights up, the sulfurous tang of the match and faint whiff of tobacco making it through the door to where I hover. Then, as I breathe in the scent of cigarette smoke, the unknown woman proceeds up the stairs, trailing ashes behind her.

Seventeen

When we have exhausted the tourist track, I drag the kids out to price bread machines.

"Have you gone completely crazy?" Tano says. "You're going to make your own bread? In *France?*"

It is rather outrageous, given that top-notch *boulangeries* dot every street in urban France.

Except where we now live.

Although I suppose it makes sense. Who ever heard of haute couture and luxury boutiques sharing space with a bakery? From our building on rue du Président Edouard Herriot, the nearest bread shop is a quarter of a mile away, which is hardly front-page news in the grand scheme of the world, but in urban France *is* somehow a shocker.

I think frequently about a little adage that hung on the wall in my favorite boulangerie in Paris: *Il vaut mieux pain sans nappe que nappe sans pain.*

In other words, food is more important than decoration... advice which clearly escaped my mind as I drooled over Amandine Fontaine's froufrou life. Just as I would never become Amandine Fontaine with her custom furnishings and stiletto heels, bread, of all things, would also prove to be elusive in this new Lyonnais life of ours.

Bread *is* life; it brings heart to a sparse meal, essential backing to a saucy one. In urban France, bread is linked to growing up, a solo trip to the boulangerie serving as a first marker of independence for many children. I can still recall Carmen, seven years old, leaving our building on rue Oberkampf, a euro clutched proudly in her hand, unknowing to this day that I was positioned at the window, monitoring every step she took past the six storefronts that stood between our building and the closest bakery.

Here on rue du Président Edouard Herriot there is no "popping out" to buy bread, no sending Carmen on this simple errand, no proposing to Lorenzo, "Would you like to go to the bakery all by *yourself* to buy a baguette?"

Now, if we want bread, we must descend the mountain and walk ten minutes—fifteen when there are crowds—to a gloomy bakery owned by one of the few crabby people I interact with in Lyon.

Emancipation from boulangerie dependency becomes pressing.

And so, it is with new bread maker clutched in my arms that I first meet the wheezing mystery woman. I hear her coming before I see her, and at first, I *shush!* the kids, thinking that the alarming lung rattle is coming from *me* as we climb the stairs; that I am having some midlife, stair-induced asthma crisis.

Until the old woman appears above us. Even coming down her breath makes a terrifying sound.

I smile. "*Bonjour, Madame!*"

She looks up from her hunched-over posture, startled. "*Bonjour?*" she answers, as though it is a question hanging between us.

She looks even older close up, with the stained, wrinkled skin—and hoarse voice—of someone who smokes several packs per day.

"We're your new neighbors," I explain, "on the fifth floor." She nods, looking a bit less mistrustful. *"Mais vous avez un très joli accent. Vous venez d'où?"*

We stand on the landing at the third floor, and I offer an abbreviated version of our family background, which she seems to approve of, because apparently she, too, adores the United States, and she also adores Argentina. (Although I will probably never cease to be surprised when the French express their love of *my* country—I have just faced too many negative attacks to ever assume that someone will be pro-United States—the French love of Argentina seems to be consistently unflappable. In the French mind, Argentina is some romantic heaven on earth.)

The woman divulges that her name is Pandora and she is a true Lyonnaise, born and raised here. In five minutes she fills us in on the diverse careers she has had since her youth, and while I won't flesh out all the details on these pages, currently she makes a living recording Edith Piaf tunes. I have trouble imagining that it's a very lucrative living, given the wretched state of her vocal cords, but then again, maybe this is one of those French-versus-Anglo questions of taste.

With our basic backgrounds out of the way, Pandora can't wait to dish out the dirt on Amandine Fontaine. Apparently she was a *salope totale*—a total bitch—of a neighbor who wouldn't loan you a cup of sugar if you begged.

"Elle était complètement prout prout," Pandora says.

Prout prout? I look to my translator for interpretation.

"Snobby, Mom," Carmen says, making a full body gesture that involves teetering around on high heel tiptoes with her nose in the air.

"*Exactement!*" Pandora is clearly delighted that this twelve-year-old wonder has managed to convey the full nuance of her point. She is also delighted that we have moved in, she tells us, even if we were certainly cheated by the owners of the building who are charging a fee for the apartment that is several hundred euros per month higher than it should be.

Oh, really?

She invites us for *apèro* that evening, and I say a little prayer that Pandora won't reveal that last piece of information about our rent to Tano.

No such luck. No sooner have we sunk into Pandora's plush velour couch (Amandine Fontaine may have been a *prout prout salope totale,* but Pandora's apartment seems to have received a heavy contribution from her decorating business) than she says, "It is disgraceful how *la famille Lamentheur* gets rich off of foreigners like you."

"*Lamentheur?*" Tano says. "But he's just the agent."

"So he says." Pandora's eyes snap with scandal. "He's the owner, and he avoids any negotiation by pretending to be 'just' a representative."

I dodge Tano's gaze as Monsieur Lamentheur's spiel—the long list of renters, how he'll fight to give *me* the apartment—floods back into my brain.

Je mens, tu mens, il ment… I lie, you lie, he lies…

It occurs to me now that "Lamentheur" could also mean "the liar."

Oh dear.

"Enough about Monsieur Lamentheur," Pandora says. "Now I will tell you about *le voisinage*."

Le voisinage is the neighbors. According to Pandora, everyone in the building is a *perdant*—loser—unfriendly, anti-social, the type to cross you in the stairway with no acknowledgment. *Ils ne disent jamais bonjour.* They never say hello.

I think back to how surprised Pandora seemed when I said hello to her, and I am fairly certain had I not spoken first, she too, would have crossed my path with nary a nod.

This comment about not saying hello seems to be a common marker for the French. I have heard countless variations on it over the years, by the French, about the French.

While we still lived in Uganda, the French members of the MSF team all said the same—people are unfriendly in France. They *never* say hello.

Parisians complain about each other. *People in such-and-such quartier never say hello.* Or, *People in our building never say hello.*

The Lyonnais I have met thus far say some variation of the same, systematically adding, *Of course nothing is as bad as in Paris!*

Yet I never have this problem. In Paris, Lyon, or anywhere else in France that I've traveled. Because I don't care what the cultural "rules"—unspoken or not—might be. I say hello to everyone. It isn't even conscious: "Hello" is a reflex. I see people in my path, I greet them. Obviously I don't salute total strangers in a bustling shopping district, for example, but if we have interacted at some point, I will say hello when we cross paths.

Admittedly, I seem to be violating some French social code that is impossible to crack. It has happened that I have said,

"*Bonjour!*" to bankers, doctors, and even my kids' teachers (this is the one that always surprises me the most) that I crossed on the street in our neighborhood, and they have stared right through me. These are people who have even been *friendly* when faced in their official context. And yet, when encountered outside, it's as though we have never met.

What compounds the confusion is that not everyone follows this code. Some French acquaintances *do* meet and greet. Since I can't keep straight who it is safe to say hello to, and who prefers the cold shoulder, I just play it safe and say hello to everyone.

This had even gotten me into trouble with Carmen, who at one stage, around the age of eight, began ordering me to keep my mouth shut whenever we approached the school grounds.

"Don't you see, Mom?" she hissed one day. "No one else's mother shouts *Bonjour! Ca va?* to everyone in sight."

I was chagrined to think that I had already, at this early age, been an embarrassment to my child. But I also disagreed. "It's not true that no one else's mother says, 'Bonjour, ça va?' I *hear* them."

"But the other mothers speak *quietly*, Mom. And French mothers are just not so…bouncy."

I was a bouncy embarrassment to my kid? *Quel horreur.* But I was also a little hurt. What was wrong with a little friendly bounce? Was the fact of growing up French going to excise that cultural trait from my daughter?

At the time, I recounted the story to my friend Leticia, a down-to-earth Toulousienne who had been in Paris for ten years, with her kids at the same school. "Well you are the only one who seems to be singing *Bonjour*, and *we* don't say *Bonjourçava* like it's one word." (Upon analysis, I took this to mean that I had created a French equivalent for that casual Americanism: *howyadoin?*)

In any event, here in Lyon this bouncy manner seems to have won Pandora over. She is now explaining that our neighborhood is known as the Carré d'Or—the Golden Square—because of its luxury boutiques and jewelry shops that stretch from place Bellecour to place des Cordeliers. Apparently, beneath the commercial façade of the quartier Cordeliers, where I have been doing the grocery shopping, lies buried history that carries all the way back past the French Revolution to the Roman Era.

I am about to remark how obscene it is that we now buy yogurt and toilet paper on the very site where so much history has played out, but Pandora announces a *pause musicale.*

She stands at her CD player and makes a little speech about Edith Piaf's life. Then she pushes the play button and the first wistful notes of "La Vie en Rose" trickle from the speakers. When the lyrics follow, at first I think it is a poor recording—the voice is flat, yet hoarse—but when I see how Pandora looks at us, so eagerly, I realize that this is one of *her* renditions.

It is touching that this strange, older woman wants to share her music with us, but I confess to having a mixed reaction to her. She has assumed a position of intimacy that feels imposing, filling our ears with negative reports of our new community, gazing at us with some sort of ethereal regard, her long golden robe giving her skin an astral glow. I cannot quite decide what, exactly, I find so strange about her, but when Carmen and I go to the bathroom we see framed newspaper articles in the hallway, and a photograph of Pandora holding a trophy.

At first I am stunned. Did she actually win some kind of music award for those tunes she croaks out?

But after peering in at the text I see that Pandora is not *only* a singer. She is also one of Lyon's most popular...*psychics?*

According to the article, Pandora has proven her clairvoyance time and again. Hence the award. My mind races through everything I have revealed while tossing back the champagne. I feel exposed. Does she know about our painful history? About my conflict around trailing Tano again? Does she already know something about the way our new life is going to turn out?

Get over it—there's nothing you can do, I tell myself, although part of me wants to race back out to the living room where Pandora perches on that *prout prout* couch and demand that she answers the question: Are we going to be okay?

My thoughts are interrupted by Carmen's giggle. "Weird," she whispers. "Pandora is a fortune teller! And it seems that she's really *good* at it."

Yet Pandora's ostensible credibility plummets when, upon our return from the bathroom, she yawps, "You *must* stop speaking English to Lorenzo. He's clearly confused."

I know that by "confused" she is referring to the fact that my son has been sitting there stuttering like crazy. Not that this is a new phenomenon. He has been stuttering, with varying degrees of severity, since he started speaking. And he started speaking later than most of his monolingual age mates. Yet experts on bilingual children say that compared to monolingual kids, multilingual kids are often delayed in speaking in full sentences. As if their little brains are busy sorting out which word goes where, and even then, as I have seen with my own kids, there is lots of mixing of languages.

I think of presenting these facts to Pandora. But deep down, I fear that the stuttering has nothing to do with Lorenzo's multilingualism and everything to do with something *I* have done wrong. A few years earlier, a French psychoanalyst friend, Hélène, whose marriage had crumbled in much the way ours had, insisted that Lorenzo's verbal issues came from my *non-dit*, all that I didn't say to Tano: about how mad I still was, how hard it was to forgive and forget, how part of me still suffered over what had transpired between us in East Africa. According to Hélène, my then three-year-old son could detect that I was repressing my feelings and that it was causing him to seize up whenever he wanted to speak. *Just like Maman.*

Of course, when I repeated this to Tano he thought that was completely hilarious: *You? Non-dit? Hélène clearly doesn't really know you.*

Still, I wasn't able to alleviate my guilt as I felt responsible in another way for Lorenzo's stutter. I thought that the time and energy I devoted to writing my first book had something to do with it.

My friends—and Tano—said this was crazy. But my self-reproach stems from the fact that when Lorenzo was one year old and just starting to speak I had gone into a book-writing obsession, under the delusion that the publication of *Trailing* would lead to financial independence. While other mothers had been singing gentle nursery songs and talking to their children in a slow, enunciated way, I had been pleading with the kids, "One more sentence! Mommy just needs to write one more sentence!" I'd send them to Susan and George's so that I could pound away at the keyboard, and although at the time it seemed perfectly reasonable—*How could it harm the kids to see their mother engaged passionately in a creative activity?*—now I wonder if my literary ambitions had come at the expense of my son's verbal development.

Pandora's voice cuts into my thoughts. "He needs to see an *orthophoniste.*"

"He already has," I counter, my words overlapping with Lorenzo's, who shouts—stutter emphatically gone—"Oh no! I *hate* orfofonistes!"

Eighteen

In the same bizarre way the French actually believe that it is cold weather that causes sore throats—hence the national obsession with scarves—they also have a fixation with *l'orthophonie*, or speech and language therapy. Every French person I've met has had at least a few sessions with an orthophoniste.

Carmen was referred to one when she was five years old (and I was heavily pregnant with Lorenzo) for a reason that was, literally, beyond my comprehension. Apparently she had an ever so slight lisp, only when speaking French, and only when she used certain words, such as *serpent* and *serpillère* ("snake" and "mop," which by the way I never heard her say, but when I asked her to, I still couldn't hear the lisp).

I couldn't say whether the sessions with the smiley, young orthophoniste corrected the ostensible lisp, but they seemed to serve as a protracted therapy for my daughter, at least as explained by the orthophoniste, who said that she and Carmen spent considerable time talking about my *grossesse* (French for pregnancy, conveniently full of S's).

Fast forward five years. Lorenzo was long out of the womb, almost six years old, but not talking much. When he did, it was sometimes like listening to a scratched album that unexpectedly hooked on a word, playing it over and over and over.

The the the the the book, he'd say (although because of his accent he'd say *Da da da da da book*).

The stutter was somehow more of a stammer, not heavy, nor consistent. Sometimes it would disappear entirely, then suddenly return for no reason we were able to discern.

Lorenzo's kindergarten teacher in Paris tried to get me to stop speaking English to him, convinced that it was the reason he struggled with his verbal communication. I explained why this would be of no useful outcome, and even detrimental to his well-being, but she assumed a dismissive attitude and referred us to an orthophoniste.

Except we said "orfofoniste," because that's how Lorenzo pronounced it, and I didn't bother correcting him. What did it matter, as long as the sessions were useful? Which I assumed they would be—or at least that he'd enjoy them as much as Carmen had.

Wrong.

He *hated* his orfofoniste, Madame Edwige Dupont, who was as commandeering and *not fun* as her name sounded.

I can't say I blamed him. I kind of hated her, too.

The minute we sat down at the first session, she bombarded Lorenzo with questions far too long and complicated for a five year old with a stutter, for God's sake: *Do you think your school canteen should serve more chocolate desserts or fruity desserts? What are your favorite games and do you prefer playing one-on-one or in a team? Do you like stories or poems better and give me some examples of both.*

Bless Lorenzo's heart, he tried to respond. But the minute he opened his mouth, Madame Edwige Dupont answered her phone, which rang incessantly. As she worked with adults with serious stuttering problems, these phone calls dragged on and on, the callers choking out their questions to her supportive coaxing. By the time she returned to us, Lorenzo lost track of what she'd asked him.

In subsequent sessions I tried to help by offering a profile of our family life. She nodded sternly, jotting notes, when I explained that Tano traveled a lot with his work. At some moment the conversation veered off into an analysis of whether Lorenzo felt nurtured.

"Well, yes," I said, surprised by the question. "We all take care of him. We all just adore him." We adored him so much, in fact, that Lorenzo had even having declared a moratorium on the word "love." We were only allowed to *like* him, not love him. He was sick and tired of all those *I love you's* we constantly showered him with. In fact, he was so sick of love that we weren't allowed to use it in his presence at all.

So when we made *crêpes au Nutella* we had to say, "mmm-mmmm, I *like* Nutella"; or when we popped in the *High School Musical* DVD for the 38th time we said we "really liked it," and at night, when I tucked him in, I could kiss and hug him with, "I like you, sweetheart."

I shared this little anecdote, thinking that it would be a good illustration of just how nurtured Lorenzo was, but Madame Dupont concluded that *this* was at the heart of his stuttering problem. Why had I been using the word "love" so much anyway, especially on a boy whose father was away much of the time? My son was clearly choking on all that love—and the eroticism that I was infusing into our relationship. It was *hyper-fusionnelle*, she admonished, not to mention borderline *érotique*, and the stutter was Lorenzo's defense, his way of saying, "*Maman*, I don't want to be your man."

Huh?

Although I don't know why I was so gob-smacked by this commentary. This idea about "fusion" was one of those buzz words that every adult in France seemed to talk about, kind of like the way in the United States everyone was always going on about self-esteem and trans-fats.

A neighbor in the Oberkampf kibbutz told me that she was taking her *two*-year-old child to see a psychologist because the child was *trop fusionnée* to her. Another friend refused to breast-feed her newborn because she believed that babies and mothers already had relationships that were far too fusionnelle. And I am still laughing at the intervention that the psychologist at the PMI (*Protection Maternelle et Infantile*, state-run maternal-child health centers) tried to stage on me, when she discovered that I was still breastfeeding Lorenzo when he was six months old.

"You have a far too fusionnelle relationship with your baby, Madame," she scolded.

"Oh good," I said.

When I saw her for a follow up when Lorenzo was a year old, and I was still breastfeeding, I thought she was going to call child protective services. After all, she chided, by continuing to offer the breast to this *person* who I may see as "my" baby but who is—as if I didn't know—a separate person, I was creating all sorts of unconscious dependencies and fixations, maybe even eating disorders.

I was tempted to say *Do you think I might cause brain damage, too?*

But instead I bit my tongue and tried to lighten up our session by recounting an anecdote I found telling of the difference in Franco and Anglo parenting trends. While the French harped on about being "too fused" with your children, the Americans I encountered couldn't stop talking about "attachment parenting."

Centered on helping children feel as secure as possible, attachment parenting does not allow distances to exist between parent and child, lest the child feel disconnected. An attachment parent will practice baby "wearing," co-sleeping, breastfeeding on demand until the child weans himself, and so on.

I was an accidental attachment parent myself, in that I breastfed both my babies until a few months past their first birthdays, and slept with them until they started sleeping through the night. Neither of these choices was because I was concerned about *their* eventual feelings—conscious or unconscious.

I was concerned about *my* feelings.

Co-sleeping meant no more staggering to pick up a screaming child at 3:00 a.m. Being right next to each other already, at the slightest peep I could insert my breast and snooze on while my baby decided how much suckling would do the job.

My sister Steph was an attachment parenting enthusiast, and one day she bubbled over the phone, "You should really try it."

At the moment she told me this, I was curled up on the sofa in our 635 square feet, the receiver pressed to one ear, my finger stuck in the other to block out noise. Lorenzo was at my feet banging his toys and Carmen was a few steps away, "feeling Argentinean" with her father's guitar.

"Attachment is our problem," I shouted over the ruckus. "We can't get any space from each other around here."

A few days after our apéro with Pandora, Tano comes home with a book in his hand. "This was in the mailbox," he says. "I think Pandora must have left it for you. Her name is written on the inside cover."

I take the book from him. "Oh, for God's sake."

It is a thin, blue volume, and from the font on the cover I don't even need to verify that it was published at least forty years earlier. *Elevée Vos Enfants avec La Langue Française,* it is called—*Raise your Children in French*—although a quick skim through makes it clear that this is written for French parents who already have a solid grasp of the language, and must therefore refer to something much more euphemistic than trying to discern between feminine and masculine nouns.

It's really quite funny how a clairvoyant know-it-all could think that using my deeply flawed French to communicate with my son, especially in such formative years, would be of any help to him. Never having been a mother herself, she also has no grasp of the impossibility for me to use any language but my own with my babies. (There is a reason it is called *mother tongue.*)

Oh Pandora, I think, sticking her silly book on a shelf where it will remain, unread. *Can't you think outside your box and see how trying to "pass" as French would erase fundamental aspects of who we are as a foreign family?*

Then I close my eyes and think that thought as strongly as I can.

Just in case she's upstairs, tuning into my brain.

Nineteen

As we move through August and toward *la rentrée*, the return to school in September, we start to meet all those people about whom Pandora warned us, the "losers who never say hello." I bombard them with Bonjourçava's? and quickly we become acquainted with the bulk of our neighbors. Like Pandora, most of them have been living in the building for thirty years, and all have something to add about la famille Lamentheur and their crooked ways. Heart pounding journeys up the 98 stairs are thereafter broken up by breath-catching stops midway, to commiserate with whatever neighbor we cross about the terribly hot weather, the mendacious owners of the building, or the filthy *parties communes*—the common areas—the two winding stairways and the courtyard below where six stinking trashcans sit, a fact I was completely blind to the day we visited the apartment.

The depressing truth—now that I see the building in clear light—is that most days, and especially *hot* days, you walk into our building and are assailed by the smell of rotting garbage. The person who is ostensibly being paid to keep this area clean looks like he is barely thirteen years old, and from the way he is dressed, one of the enslaved children from the nearby Roumanian gypsy settlements, whose expulsions are causing polemic all over Europe.

A few times a week he straggles up the stairs with a half bucket of brackish water and a filthy rag that he sort of swishes around on the floor as he makes his way back to the bottom. Lorenzo has taken to scampering up the stairs on hands and knees, and the color of his palms and pants by the time we make it to our door is all the proof needed that the current cleaning system is *not* working.

One particularly humid afternoon Lorenzo drags himself up the steps, almost slithering on his belly, ignoring my repeated request that he stand up and walk. When he suddenly says, "Oh YUCK!" and I see the sticky glob of saliva gooping from his hand, I lose my temper.

"Get up!" I hiss, grabbing him by the shirt and yanking him to a stand. Some combination of the fact that a phlegmy blob has been deposited in our stairway, and that my disobedient child now has some tubercular filth on his hands... Well, let's just say that I can no longer contain the weeks of my own pent-up tension.

"I cannot wait for school to start!" I shriek.

And this is true. I have been gazing longingly at *ECOLE LAMARTINE*, our neighborhood's public elementary school, every time we step out of our apartment. It is right down the street, sandwiched between place des Jacobins and place des Célestins, where there is a beautiful old theater set back in a tree-lined plaza. I see the school, where Lorenzo will begin first grade, through my American lens, where old French architecture looks quaint and romantic, and in this case specifically, like it has been lifted right out of the *Madeline* books (save for the fact that it is not covered in vines, nor is it "at" Paris, as Lorenzo will not stop reminding me).

The day before school starts we actually make it inside the building. This is no small feat for a French elementary school, as during the school year the doors are locked to prevent kids getting out, or parents getting in. Only the teachers are in the building that day, getting ready for the arrival of their students, and we slip through the doors like spies. Hanging on the bulletin board are the classroom assignments. Lorenzo's classroom is on the third floor and we creep up the echoey stairs, which are of the same steep proportion as those in our building, freezing in our steps and finally turning and running, hand in hand, when we hear voices descending toward us. Mission aborted.

That night at dinner I try to make light-hearted conversation about our adventure. "Do you want to tell Pop what you thought of your new school?" I ask Lorenzo.

"It's fucking shit," he says.

"Lorenzo!"

Tano sniffs. "No question who he learned that from, is there?"

The next day I leave the house early with Carmen while Tano and Lorenzo have breakfast. I have to get Carmen to the nearby school bus stop, for she has been given a place at a school a few miles away, the *Cité Scolaire Internationale*, a French school with nine international sections (Anglo, German, Japanese, Chinese, Polish, Arabic, Portugese, Spanish and Italian) in which students receive, in addition to the regular French curriculum, six hours of mother-tongue level instruction in literature and social studies in the section they are enrolled. Carmen looks adorable in her skinny jeans and the sequined book bag that all the girls in Paris tote, but she fidgets with her hair and whispers, "I'm nervous, Mom."

I give her hand a squeeze. Of course she's nervous. Everything is new. She's never ridden a school bus before, she's never attended an international school.

We have seen the school already. The day we got the phone call that her application was accepted, we went to visit and ended up getting an impromptu and personalized orientation from an older student about where she needed to go on the first day—a day, the student assured us, no cool kid would come with their parents. Now as the bus approaches I wonder if it was a mistake to not go with her. But too late. In one screech of the brakes the vehicle has stopped before us, Carmen barely waves good-bye, and she disappears into the belly of the bus, where I can hear shouts of laughter and chatter.

Back at the apartment Tano and Lorenzo are waiting for me downstairs. Lorenzo has a big scowl on his face. We escort him to Ecole Lamartine and proceed up the stairs, all together, the first day of school being the one day that parents are allowed in without special permission. *At least we've been training for this all summer,* I think, as I count 79 stairs from the entrance to his classroom. Will the shorter climb perk Lorenzo up?

It doesn't.

Nor does the fact that his classroom looks like a preserved model of a classroom from World War II. Wooden benches line the back walls, and each student's desk is of the pulpit variety. I am instantly charmed, and turn to whisper to Tano. But something else has caught his eye. "Can you get a load of this crowd?" he whispers.

My eyes skim the group. Had it been possible to strip away the aesthetics of the ultra-wealthy, and all their material trappings—the Manolo Blahnik heels, the Vuitton bags, the Cartiers and Rolexes—we are just another group of hovering parents. But as this *is* the elementary school of the Carré d'Or, it is par for the course that we are surrounded by women with puffy, siliconed lips, perky boob jobs, and some outfits that must cost more than our monthly rent.

God, even some of the *fathers* look like they've had work done.

With parents like these it is only natural that the boys in this class—with names that sound so stuffy to my Anglo ears, like Algernon, and Clement, and Gaston—are polished into little men, with preppy haircuts, button-down Lacoste shirts, cable knit sweaters draped neatly over their six-year-old shoulders. Even their Superga tennies are spit-spot clean.

Now picture our Lorenzo, three inches taller than all these delicate little French boys. For his first day of school he has insisted on wearing his favorite jeans (too short and ripped at the knees) and a faded skateboard T-shirt. His uncombed hair looks like a rough and tumble mess. He is our gorgeous, strapping boy, he is—but what he isn't, is *coiffed*.

Fucking shit, indeed, I think, glancing down at my own casual garb: Worn jeans, a T-shirt, my favorite gold-colored flip-flops. I think back to earlier in the week. "No offense, Mom," Carmen said, "But don't you think you should stop wearing that kind of outfit around here?"

I pooh-poohed her comments (*Oooooh la la*, I believe I said, *aren't you the prout-prout mademoiselle?*) but now looking around I realize that I do look, ummmm, rather sloven compared to everyone else crammed into this hallway.

Suddenly the buzzing of the parents and children falls quiet. The teacher has arrived. Madame Dubois is a sluggish older woman with drooping eyelids who starts the meeting by informing the children that they may speak only when given permission. Then she turns to us parents, huddling on the periphery of the classroom, and says that she hopes we will work with our kids to help them understand the rules: in particular, speak only when spoken to. As an aside she adds that she is ten months from retirement and it could not come a day too soon.

"Holy shit," I mutter to Tano as we leave the meeting. "Whatever happened to 'Welcome to school, kids! Learning is fun'?"

He laughs. "Don't worry. It will be fine."

At home later that morning I scrub the marble floor—*again*, trying to extract years' worth of grime from the stones' pores—and think about what is ahead. I pray Lorenzo's day is going okay.

Pray that he is comfortable with his classmates and that Madame Dubois is not as much of a stooge-pot as she seemed in that sorry excuse for a meeting.

Pray that he is having a day where he can speak without stuttering, because I know: If the words aren't coming easy, he won't speak at all.

Mostly I just pray that he is happy to exist. I will start my two-day commute to Paris in ten days, and I honestly cannot stand the idea of leaving him while he is so blue.

When I am done with the floors I take a damp rag and start in on the radiators, their grooves caked with sticky dust. Lorenzo's chagrin seems commingled with my own, past and present, and I find it hard to know how much to worry, how much to protect, and how much to just let go.

At 4:30, I trade my Levi's for a fancier brand of jean, my flip-flops for leather sandals, and go in search of my son.

Twenty

None of my prayers have been heard. Lorenzo's day was awful, he says, and he hates the school. Hates the teacher. Hates the other kids.

"I just want to go back at Paris," he says, fighting tears as we trickle out of the courtyard with the crowd. He tugs me in the direction of our apartment, but I take note of the throngs of elegant mothers gravitating to place des Célestins.

"I know, sweetheart," I say, dragging him in the direction of the crowd, feeling a tad intimidated myself. "But today we can't go to Paris. Today we're going over here."

The benches of the square are adorned with gorgeous women in stylish, form-fitting clothes, chatting on iPhones, chatting with each other, smoking cigarettes, passing out *goûters* (snack) to their children. One edge of the plaza is occupied by an ornate, gilt-trimmed theater, its steps dotted with more of the same: svelte, beautiful women, lounging around while they supervise their children.

I feel like I am in a James Bond movie with the mothers of Célestins as mysterious, desirable Bond girls.

I watch, mesmerized, as they chase after toddlers in their high, strappy heels, the skirts of their flouncy dresses lifting gently to show perfectly toned legs and smooth, bronzed skin. My senses actually flood, the sound of husky feminine voices, murmuring their stories to each other or trilling the rules to the children, the smooth swish of their light-as-feather wisps of clothing, the musky scent of expensive perfume. I am aware that in my casual attire I do not blend in, and that the sexual titillation I feel observing these gorgeous women counteracts the stand I took long ago to shrug off all of those image pressures. Part of me suddenly feels that old yearning to provoke, to be sexually tantalizing, too. God, has my stance all this time been intellectual without a corollary emotional base?

I contemplate this while a forlorn Lorenzo eats his pain au chocolat I bought from Pignol. The act of biting into my own flaky croissant clears the sensual scrim through which I have been surveying the scene, and I can see a familiar group of boys in Lacoste busily beating the bushes with a stick.

"Look! Those boys are in your class. Why don't you go say hi?"

Lorenzo's eyes fill with tears again. "I don't know how to make friends, Mom."

I rub his back. My poor, sad baby. I coach him on walking up to someone, *anyone*, that he recognizes, and saying, "*Je m'appelle Lorenzo.*"

But he refuses, and eventually we go home, his head hanging.

Carmen's school year, on the other hand, has gotten off to a roaring good start. On day one she's made a bunch of friends, all of whom are bicultural, bilingual, and new to Lyon as well. She does not even want to be escorted to the bus stop again, and goes bounding out the door full of enthusiasm every morning that week.

Lorenzo, however, has to be dragged out of bed. He begs me to let him stay at home, tears glistening in his eyes as he says, "Madame Dubois is *soooooo* mean."

I am alarmed. The French educational system is notorious for its severe classroom culture, built largely around the practice of debasement and humiliation of the student. Lorenzo, thus far, has never had any truly mean teachers—crabby, maybe, but not cruel—but then again, he has only ever been in the pre-kindergarten and kindergarten program until now.

Carmen, who also entered the French school system at age three, has had some incredibly lovely teachers over the years, but has also been subjected to the culture of insults and inhumanity ostensibly reserved for those students who are not doing well in school. Carmen has always been a naturally good student, and even she has had "*Tu ne sers à rien*,"—"You're useless"—snapped at her when she struggled with certain grammatical or mathematic concepts.

What I find amazing in France is that *la malaise française* is an active topic of debate. The public polemic goes round and round: *Why are French people so unhappy? Why are they so negative? Why does the French population consume more anti-depressants and anti-anxieties than any other European nation?*

To me it seems rather obvious that all this national gloom and doom must somehow relate back to the punitive, critical educational system. Even if a kid is lucky enough to avoid this type of condemning teacher throughout his school career, the chance that he is being raised by parents who were victims of mean teachers is, nonetheless, very high. The punitive educational style dates back so many generations that there are few people to have made it through to adulthood without having dealt with a cruel teacher. This is not to say that French parents are mean. Rather, it is to say that adult victims must internalize it so deeply that no matter their own parenting style, at some level, they must find it natural for their own kids to suffer the same.

As an outsider, however, none of this feels normal, including the fact that my once-exuberant six year old is so miserable at school. But Tano points out that it is not fair to immediately assume that Madame Dubois is as horrible as Lorenzo says. Could it be that Lorenzo has a bad attitude?

Lorenzo? My love, Lorenzo?

Although my gut reaction to this proposition is that Tano has sided with the enemy—*traitor!*—constant guilt over the apartment tames me into offering a more measured response. The last thing I want is to get onto opposing sides with Tano over something as important as this, even though deep down I feel that as Mom I have a special, symbiotic understanding of my children.

"Ok," I say. "I'll work with him on his attitude."

It becomes my project to infuse my morose charge with positivity, to cheer him on and convince him that everything will be okay.

Lorenzo picks at his breakfast one morning while I sing, "*You've got to ac-cen-tu-ate the positive!*" But he resists my zeal and I practically have to force him down the sidewalk to Ecole Lamartine, extolling a chipper optimism that I don't really feel, hugging him good-bye so tightly that he says, "Mom!"

But as I loosen my hold I notice that he doesn't, he holds on, and says, in a small voice, "Don't leave me here, Mom."

His plea stirs a feeling of such unalloyed love, abruptly followed by a cold bucket of worry as the bell rings. I pry his fingers from around my waist and prod him into the school.

Inside I'm filled with anxiety, less about the misery of this particular morning, but about my impending departure. I cannot go back to Paris and leave my kid in this dour state. I have got to fix this situation.

At the end of the day, and every day thereafter that week, Lorenzo's expression remains long. Still, every afternoon I force him to Célestins in a quest to help him make friends. It is a pursuit that is not going well, for he remains glued to me, talking about Paris.

I try to attend to his melancholy, but I feel in a cloud myself, these afternoons, sitting on the sidelines observing. I may have lived in one of the most fashion conscious, vain cities of the world for ten years, but the maze of my life in Paris rarely intersected with the people that make up *this* crowd: primped, pressed, buffed, powdered, blown dry and absolutely *maintained*.

Who are these women?

There is the Louis Vuitton plastic surgery trio, whose frail ankles and age-spotted hands give them away as much older women who waited until the very last minute to produce their children. These mothers gleam wealth. It's hard to describe, really, and I cannot understand how they always manage to look so photo-shoot perfect, no-detail spared, day in and day out, while managing small—often screaming—children.

Then there are the women who seem to have it all, the ones who stride into Célestins in their perfectly tailored suits, four-inch heels, elegant briefcases in hand. I have no idea what they do for a living, but whatever it is, they look absolutely fabulous doing it. I must say, though, that if anyone exudes an air of "let's not say hello to each other," it is this group.

The whole lot of Célestins mothers reminds me of James Bond girls, true, but there is a particular trio amongst the crowd—the trio I am most drawn to—that I think of as the Charlie's Angels. Why? Because there are three of them, and they are always together, and when I see them I feel how I felt when I was a kid watching the TV show: mesmerized, envious, curious, and most of all, as if I could never actually *be* like them.

The "leader" of the Charlie's Angels of place des Célestins is a beautiful blonde, with small, neat features, save for that classic French protruding upper lip that on anyone but a sultry French woman would be an untreated overbite. She is stunningly sexy: with her stick thin frame she has the appearance of a rocker. She always dresses in skin-tight clothes that look like they have been painted on, and transparent T-shirts, never a bra underneath. That she can flounce around in public with her nipples showing and appear completely unbothered is fascinating.

Her two best friends are less obviously beautiful, but alluring in a jolie-laide way. The redhead has pale skin and almost gaunt features, giving her the bedroom look of someone who has been screwing a lover for twenty-four hours straight and just realized that she needed to eat something.

The brunette keeps her hair short, in a style that flatters her dark skin and strong features. She has this provocative way of sweeping the wisps of her hair back behind her ears, always adorned with big gold Cartier hoops.

Although I have already chatted with different members of the James Bond after-school community, so far I have not exchanged a single word with the Charlie's Angels. But through observation alone I can discern a few things about them:

1.) They seem to have gobs of money, as noted by the purchases they arrive with at snack time and hold up for each other's approval, filmy articles of silk and satin from the most chic stores of the Carré d'Or;

2.) They all smoke—Gitanes, no less, to complete their iconic image—and though I cannot be sure, I suspect that there is the occasional joint passing among them;

3.) They all have sons in Lorenzo's class. The blonde's son is Victor, the redhead has Boniface, and the brunette's is Jean-Claude.

Amidst all this pomp and glamour, Lorenzo and I turbo eat pastries on the steps of the theater. I check out the women, and he sneaks glimpses at the boys, whose daily after-school project involves constructing a cabin in the bushes, swinging from the trees, and periodically breaking into kung fu fighting attacks.

"Please, my darling," I plead. "Let's go meet those guys. I'll go with you. The hardest part is walking up to them. After that it will be okay. I *promise.*"

But he refuses, and we go home every night that week feeling pretty damn terrible, him wishing he didn't exist and me hating myself for not having the answers.

One night I toss and turn in bed so much that Tano finally flips on the light and squints at me. "Is something wrong?"

"I'm worried about the kids."

"Why? They're doing great."

I glare at him, although admittedly, Carmen *is* in top form. The verdict has not changed: She *adores* being in the international program of her new school. For the first time in her life, English is the language of her school friendships, the fact of which appears to have yanked the seal off of some formerly buried side of herself. Gone is the rather shy, quiet child who had once lamented being misunderstood by everyone in her life—French and Anglo alike. That child has been replaced by a garrulous, confident young teenager who seems to be reveling in the discovery that there are all of these age mates with whom she shares an international identity, kids who comprehend, without having to have anything explained to them, all the ways that she *isn't* French, in spite of any appearances to the contrary.

As I make her breakfast one morning, she tells me she feels that now she, too, "belongs" to a community in a way that she rarely has before; that being at Cité Scolaire Internationale is like suddenly knowing a whole world of Susans and Georges and Matthews—our fellow foreign family friends of the first floor, rue Oberkampf. I am touched by this discovery, for if in France our kids have always been able to pass as "local" in a way that Tano and I cannot, this very fact has, in turn, created a certain cultural gap between us and our children. That Carmen is now immersed in a community of international kids makes her childhood look a lot more similar to mine, and some of the cultural difference between us has shortened.

"You're right—about Carmen," I reply. "She's doing great. It's Lorenzo I'm worried about. He hates school, and no matter what I do it's not getting any better."

"According to Lorenzo."

"What? You don't believe him?"

"It's not that I don't believe him. I'm just not convinced that you're getting the full story."

"Maybe not the full story, but it looks like there is no attention to the happiness factor…"

He cuts me off. "How do you know that? Are you spying outside the classroom door every day?"

"I think it was pretty obvious from that first meeting. Not to mention Lorenzo's feedback."

"Listen, Querida, it's not a teacher's job to pay attention to every detail of a kid's happiness. That's your cultural bias."

Damn straight it's a cultural bias! I feel like screaming. Tano has always been defensive of the French system, which he finds far more compatible with the Argentinean one, in terms of content. We have had many a squabble over the years when he points out how surprised he is at how little Americans seem to know about history and science—his lovely wife included.

Whether the US system is not well-rounded is hard for me to judge, given that I grew up in the international school system (based largely, I admit, on the US curriculum). From what I understand of my own experience, as well as critiques I've read of the different systems, the US approach to education is based less on rote memorization of facts and more on learning to think creatively.

Besides, it annoys me that Tano is defensive of the Madame Dubois's of the world. I know he appreciates the French system because he works with so many smart French people that he admires, and it somehow reaffirms his belief in the cultural system that he was raised in. On the other hand, there is no "Argentinean malaise" the way there is a "French malaise," no culture of hyper-negativity in Argentina the way there is in France. So even if the Argentinean system demands more rote memorization and less creative thinking than the US system it is highly unlikely that the teacher drilling the facts into the student's heads is informing them that they are useless blobs with nary a brain cell.

"Just relax," Tano yawns, in a tone that I know is meant to be reassuring but that sends a surge of irritation pulsing through my veins. "He'll be fine."

Easy for you to be cavalier, I think. Tano is as Zen as I have ever seen him. He's got a great job, the wife and kids are back, and he rides his fantastic sports bike back and forth to work, more of a hard body than ever, fit as a fiddle at age fifty while I become lardier than I have ever been in my life.

That's another reason I'm testy these days: because I am not feeling *bien dans ma peau*—good in my skin—as the French say, and my afternoon gawk sessions of the trim mothers at Célestins are not helping. I have this distant vision of myself—brassy, energetic, svelte—standing before the newly arrived crowd of trailing spouses at the American Church of Paris's *Bloom Where You're Planted* program.

I speak so knowingly about the stress of moving a family and how it is of utmost importance to keep self-care in mind. *Enjoy France's wine,* I say. *Just not too much. And enjoy the culture of food—just make sure it's in moderation. Emotional eating and drinking is never a solution.*

Then I tell the story of a former client who came to Paris and only realized how stressed out she actually was when the button popped off her pants as she walked past the Eiffel Tower.

Well, *hello,* I think now. My metaphoric button pops with every sweet treat I snarf. I feel anything but sylphlike after the stress of these past months. And lest this seem like dysmorphic whining, the fact that I am actually chunking up is a disturbing reflection of my *mood.* Once light, now heavy.

Yet I cannot control my urge to splurge—on calories, that is—every time I feel, well, *anything.* "Emotional eating" is an understatement for what is happening to me. Sad? Pop in to Pignol. Happy? Pop in to Pignol. Not sure how I feel today? Pop in to Pignol.

What I have been doing might be best defined as rapid-fire caloric inhalation. And what exactly have I inhaled? Millefeuilles, Paris-Brests, financiers, canelés, divorcés, croissants aux amandes, moelleux au chocolat… And oh! Best of all: the discovery of the *real* way to eat fromage frais—sprinkled with sugar and doused in heavy, sweet cream.

Tano snores by now, lifting me from my gourmet reverie. I study his face in the dim light—*How can he be so relaxed when I feel so hysterical? Doesn't he get affected by the kid's hardships the way I do? Does he even notice without me here to point it out?*

And then I think of another thing to worry about: *What the hell will go down when we reverse roles?*

My mind reaches back almost a year when I went to London for a weekend's training. Tano arrived early from Lyon that day to be in charge of the kids. I had stocked the fridge and cupboards for their weekend together and thought lovingly of my husband while I Eurostarred under the English Channel. By that evening, however, after having called Tano repeatedly and getting no answer, my affectionate thoughts turned catastrophic. Finally, in desperation, I called Susan and George, who went upstairs to check.

A minute later my phone rang. "You need me?" Tano's harried voice came over the line.

"I've been calling you since *lunchtime*. Why don't you answer?"

"I haven't had a minute to myself. There's all the meals, and the kitchen clean up, and then one kid needs help with this, the other needs help with that—"

Oh, so now he finally gets it. "Don't forget the laundry," I chirped. "You'll need to get to that too, you know."

When I got home from London, the apartment was a mess, Tano looked bedraggled, his hair unwashed and his beard, normally well-tended, somehow gone scraggly.

"Are you alright?" I asked, alarmed by his chaotic demeanor.

"How do you do it?" he asked. And then, grudgingly, as though I had held out on some domestic top secret, added, "You must have a *system*."

A system? Try some good old-fashioned structure, the concept that for years I had fought for and he had avoided, landing it at the heart of most of our squabbles about anything related to the children.

He looked so awful, though, so mowed down, that at that moment I hadn't had the heart to criticize or lay on a round of "I told you so."

Instead I began the clean up process, barking orders at the kids and the man, all three of whom sprang to action, clearly relieved that General Mommy was back in action.

A car alarm shrills from place Bellecour, obscenities are shouted, and my connection to the past is broken. I turn off the bedside light and try to calm myself, but to no avail. How can I leave for Paris? How will Tano ever manage the kids? Am I selfish to hang on to my professional life? Am I compromising the kids' well-being by attending to my own?

Do I even want to do this?

In my mind's eye I can see my little office as though it were yesterday that I turned the lock for the summer. But I feel entirely removed, as though that was some other life, some other incarnation of myself. If someone called me tomorrow to say that the whole thing had burned down and that all my clients had found a new therapist, part of me would be relieved.

I drift off to sleep on a sea of troubled thoughts.

The next day is the last school day before I am to leave for Paris.

That afternoon, Lorenzo and I sit on the steps of Célestins, watching the boys play in the bushes while their sexy mothers loll around nearby. At one moment a scuffle breaks out and two girls who look like they're about Lorenzo's age run up to the steps where their moms sit.

"She rubbed mud on me!" one girl cries.

"Did not!"

"Did too!"

"Did not! And anyway, your dress is ugly!"

"It's not ugly. It's *Dior*."

I find this exchange so remarkable that I text Deanna: *From the mouths of babes at the Carré d'Or: Don't get mud on my Dior.*

She answers: *Have you taken up poetry?*

I turn back to Lorenzo. "*Please*," I plead, "Let's find a way to talk to those guys."

But when he refuses again, I pull out the big guns. "If you go over there and talk to those boys, when I get back from Paris I will take you to the toy store and you can pick a special present."

In a flash he is gone, straight to the bushes where the crowd opens up as though they've just been waiting for him. I even hear one of the boys call him by name.

We stay at Célestins until nightfall. It is still summer hours and it stays light until late. By 6:00 p.m. most of the children and their Goddess mothers have fallen away and it is just us mortal hangers-on that remain, likely, it seems, united in the fact that we have boys that need to run off enough of their energy to make it bearable to go back to our apartmented lives, where there will always be neighbors downstairs to complain about the thuds and bangs of wild horseplay. Winter will be hell.

But for now, Célestins is ours, and we move to the side of the stairs when the theater goers in their handsome attire begin to appear, our little devils still rattling happily in the bushes.

Twenty-One

The day before I leave for Paris, I buzz around the supermarket at place des Cordeliers and the open-air market on the quai du Rhône, buying every food item I can think of that my family might want in my absence. When all three freezer drawers heave vegetarian lasagnas and pizzas and frozen peas and ice cream, and the fridge bulges with milk and yogurt and apple sauce and vegetables and lentils with cumin and coconut cream, the way Carmen, especially, likes it, and the fruit bowl brims apples and peaches and kiwis, I realize that I don't have enough flour to make another loaf of bread, and I practically hyperventilate.

Carmen comments, "No offense, Mom, but do you *really* think we're going to eat all of that while you're gone?"

And so, bread unbaked, the next day I leave. It is late Sunday afternoon and I have booked myself into the Cosmos, the best-kept secret of a hotel right up the street from the Oberkampf kibbutz. But dinner that night is *chez moi*, or rather, chez the family from Kent State University who live chez moi, who have invited me—and all the neighbors—for apéro.

I drop my bag at the hotel and wander over to our building, feeling oddly disconnected as I punch in the door code and enter the courtyard. But time peels back as I spot the traces of my own children—toys they have left behind, Lorenzo's old tricycle, Carmen's jump rope—and my heart leaps into my throat.

How strange it is to come "home," to live out the possibility of *return*. Of all the places my lifetime has stretched across outside of the United States, this is the only place that I have ever returned to. So *this* is what it is like to "go back to," to have your personal history remain accessible, for visitation, as a touchstone. This is what it will be like, to come and go, as I plan to, secure in the knowledge that some version of my old life will always be waiting here.

I go up the stairs, past Susan and George's, to the third floor where our names are still on the door, next to the little witch sticker that Carmen stuck there at least five Halloweens ago. Inside many neighbors are already seated, glasses of wine in hand. I kiss and hug people hello and my eyes travel around the little apartment the way my mind travels back in time. I feel like a kid who has returned from camp after a long summer away. For months I had suppressed this ache for the familiar, yet being here now, as the guest in my own home, my heart gets skittery, and I down my first glass of wine practically in a single gulp.

What has happened in my absence? There is a brand new baby in the building—her name, Louise, kept a surprise until now. She is not named after me, but her parents know that I will be delighted at their choice. The other kids of the building, my children's friends, clamor for their turn to tell me what's happened since we last saw each other: fingers have been broken, teeth lost, training wheels removed from bikes. I pull little notes and drawings that Carmen and Lorenzo have made for their old pals, and distribute them to eager hands. I knew that these kids would be ready with something for me to take back to Lyon, and I receive their crumpled cards, their private notes marked TOP SECRET, with great care.

More wine flows. I see how happy the family from Kent State seems to be: how they have jumped right into life on the kibbutz. Their daughter is already good friends with Matthew, and from the exchange of inside jokes I can tell that this is not the first gathering of neighbors since we left in July.

Susan wedges herself into the love seat size sofa next to me and whispers, "Is this hard?"

Time curves back over this beautiful chapter of my life, the Paris chapter, so much of which played out right here, where we are all now gathered. After just a few months in the bigger space in Lyon part of me already marvels at how we had managed to live in such a small apartment for so many years. I remember vividly the tumult, how we always seemed to be on top of each other, the noise and the chaos and the closeness.

I lean into Susan. "No, it's not hard," I say, and as I do I am aware of this nascent shift inside me. "It feels good to see that everything has worked out so well."

Later, back at the hotel, I call our apartment in Lyon. It is just after 10:30. Carmen answers on the third ring and immediately I can hear Lorenzo hooting in the background, the strains of guitar music competing with his voice.

"You're *all* still up?"

"We just finished dinner," she reports.

"Just *now*?"

"Well Pop did bricolage all evening and then he took us roll-erblading. We went all the way to Parc de la Tête d'Or!"

I had prepared all that food so that the kids would not be on South American schedule on a school night. Silly me. I mean, why have an early dinner and call it a day on a Sunday night when you can go rollerblading?

But how can I be annoyed? Carmen sounds absolutely exhilarated by the rollerblading adventure, and it is only thanks to Tano's handyman skills that our apartment is finally taking shape. Since moving in he has spent every spare waking minute doing bricolage. He bought and installed light fixtures in every room. He sanded, stained, and mounted a beautiful oak counter in the kitchen, and found a gorgeous set of cabinets to match. He put shelves and mirrors in both bathrooms. And though it had become immediately clear that without the interior decorator's budget and eye, we were never going to replicate Amandine Fontaine's fancy home, Tano's meticulous fixing up had slowly but surely transformed the cursed place into something liveable, even pleasant.

Of course, he could have fed the kids while he was doing bricolage—that's what I would have done—but that is probably the most important cultural particularity of Tano: meals must always be *shared*. In my casual American system, each person can eat when they are hungry. What matters is getting nourished. How many times had I gotten the kids settled at the table and then bustled around them, multi-tasking other chores and maybe even nibbling along with them, without once ever sitting down?

For Tano, the nourishment is as much in the shared company as the food. Of course they'd eat together, and no matter if the schedule he "planned" wouldn't have them fed until 10:00 p.m.

"Let me talk to him," I say.

"Paaapaaaa!" she hollers. The guitar music abruptly stops. I hear him say, "Lorenzo, *anda sepillar tus dientes.*" Go brush your teeth. Then, to me, "Can I call you later? I'm just getting the kids ready for bed."

I glance at my watch. 10:55! On a school night! I start to say something, but as I do, another thought fills my head: *I only feel Argentinean when I play the guitar.*

Eating late, prioritizing music and relationships over time-table…this is also the kids' education, about who their father is, and by extension, who they are.

Just before midnight I call him back, half expecting to hear Lorenzo running around. But when Tano answers all I can hear in the background are the wistful strains of a violin.

"I'm ironing," he says.

"I know," I say, and I do, because he always turns on the classical music station when he irons. We chat about the evening and then I say, "Was Lorenzo anxious about school tomorrow?" I fully expect a dismal report.

"I don't think so," Tano says. "If he was he didn't say anything about it."

"Nothing?"

"Well, let's see. He told me about the Ninja versus Samurai game he is playing with some other kids at every recess, and he told me that he hopes there is mousse au chocolat at the canteen tomorrow. That's about it. Oh! And he went to bed in his own room tonight."

"How on earth did you manage that?"

"It was his idea. And by the time he got into bed he was so tired he went straight to sleep."

So, Carmen, Lorenzo, and Tano are all fine. Life did not go to hell in my absence. Am I a narcissist for thinking it would, or just completely neurotic?

Because maybe this was all just a projection.

Maybe the biggest surprise is that back here in Paris, in my little hotel, *I* am fine, too. I haven't gone to pieces embarking on my new commuter life, I haven't tried to micromanage every breath my family takes, and I truly enjoyed being a guest in my own apartment.

And so with nothing more to report, we get off the phone. I need to be in my office at 9:00 a.m., and I realize, as I set the alarm, that without the kids to make breakfast for and escort to school, I don't need to get up nearly as early as I normally do. Who'd have thought it took going back to work to get to sleep in a little bit?

Lying in the dark, I feel oddly invigorated. I think about my little exchange with Susan: *It feels good to see that everything has worked out so well.* And that sentiment covers every aspect of my life right now: the one I left behind and the one we are re-designing.

The next morning I go down for breakfast in the hotel lobby. The croissants are flaky and warm, and I smear them with spoonfuls of sweet strawberry jam from the farmer's market on

Boulevard Richard Lenoir—the same one I went to twice a week for ten years. At the tables around me are other professionals—I can tell by their calendars, Blackberries, and laptops—and I am filled with a renewed sense of belonging and purpose. I used to live and work in Paris; now I am back home for work.

I have a third cup of coffee and leave for the office.

Twenty-Two

And so begins our role reversal. Tano rarely travels at all anymore, yet I leave the nest every Sunday evening, returning home Tuesday night. It is a protracted family therapy, with Tano coming to terms with what it means to work full time and be on his own with the kids, and my learning about what it means to *let go*; to accept that I am no longer fully in charge, to let Tano have his own rhythm with our children that will allow them to appreciate and resent him for his own merits or shortcomings.

Yet, if at first it is exhilarating to commute to Paris for work, defying, I believe, a second round of trailing spousedom, rapidly the quality of my own life seems to be diminishing.

I have *no time* anymore.

No matter the hour I arrive back in Lyon on Tuesday nights, Wednesdays always start early. Carmen has to be up at 7 to make the school bus, and I rise with her to make her breakfast and catch up on the last couple of days. As soon as she leaves, I rouse Lorenzo to get him to le Skate Park at parc de Gerland where he is taking an *atelier skateboard*. (Prior to 2013, elementary age kids in France didn't have school on Wednesdays, and middle schoolers only a half day.) Then we race home so that I can get both kids fed before Carmen has to be escorted to her guitar lessons, twenty minutes away at a totally inconvenient time that I agreed to only because she begged (and I wanted to help her feel Argentinean).

I don't mean to sound peevish, because honestly, these mother-child reconnections are a highlight of my week. The problem, though, is that I am having trouble relaxing, ever, because of the *mess*, generated in two days—heaps of laundry, dirty floors, dust and clutter....

God how I miss a small apartment.

Nights in bed in Lyon I flop back in exhaustion, looking at Tano out of the corner of my eye. Usually he does sudoku—*niveau diabolique*—chewing his lip in concentration and paying me no mind whatsoever, other than periodically pressing his chilly toes companionably onto my leg.

It has taken less time than I even imagined for us to revert to old married couple status. In other words, the aphrodisiacal quality of the weekend marriage model has gone completely missing in the Mommy-is-now-the-commuter model, in which I feel, among other things, erotically numb.

To care or not to care?

That *is* the question.

In theory, I feel a whole range of nostalgic yearnings for our old lusty selves.

In reality, now I am so knackered it is a relief that Tano seems as entirely unstimulated by my carnal presence as I am by his. We do curl up like spoons to sleep, and most mornings when I wake we are still wrapped in each other's arms. But now instead of groping and clutching each other the five evenings per week that we are together, he tries to concentrate on his sudoku while I try to get him to agree with me that the French educational system is quite possibly destroying our son's self esteem. (I admit it: I *am* one of those Americans.)

"Lorenzo is playing you for sympathy. He *never* complains about school when you're not here."

That's because you have him outside playing soccer and eating late night ice cream cones every time I leave town, I think, although I refrain from saying this lest it sound like a critique. Which of course it is although I have to accept that the joy Lorenzo gets from these father-son moments more than compensates for the lack of structure that I worry about.

"Have you ever thought," Tano adds, "about the power of suggestion?"

"Meaning?"

"Meaning that when you keep asking Lorenzo how he's doing, you keep referring to his supposed misery."

"Well what am I supposed to do? He keeps telling me about it!"

"Do what I do," Tano says. "Give him a hammer and a nail and ask him to help you."

Not that I am ever doing anything with a hammer and nail, but I get Tano's point. Not only has he recruited both kids into many of his bricolage projects—tasks they seem to really enjoy—but together they have embarked on all sorts of creative constructions based on the kids specific requests. In Lorenzo's case, the desire was to build a skate park for his finger sized skate boards, and Carmen requested her father's assistance to construct an adorable necklace holder, followed by a bulletin board made from wine-bottle corks (giving Mommy a perfect excuse to drink).

I tell Tano that I will hold back on all this poor-Lorenzo-hates-school business if he will agree to attend the meeting with Madame Dubois that I organized for Friday morning.

That Friday we sit before Madame Dubois, who looks positively exhausted, so much so that I feel almost sheepish for having gotten her to school a half hour earlier than the starting bell. But there we are, so I explain that Lorenzo seems to be struggling, and that I am also concerned about whether he is stuttering…

"How would I know?" Madame Dubois cuts me off. "He never says a word. He is *complètement dans les nuages.*"

Apparently Lorenzo is "in the clouds," checked out completely, and I do not appreciate the tone in which this information is conveyed—as though he is to blame and she has no role to play in engaging him.

"Give her a break," Tano says after the meeting. He can see how pissed off I am. "She's old. She's tired. She's about to retire."

"Don't you find it a bit strange how she just declared that he never says a word?"

"She has *thirty-two* six year olds to deal with. She must be elated that he never says a word."

ARGH! I want to scream. How can we just accept this?

"Look," Tano adds. "I know it's not great. Clearly she's not the most inspirational teacher ever. But you can't say it's all going wrong. Look at how well Lorenzo is reading."

I have to admit he has a point. Madame Dubois is using a phonetic method called *La Planète des Alphas*—Alpha Planet—to teach the kids to read. Twenty-six wacky characters, each with a series of distinct jobs and sounds, live on this planet. It is one thing that Lorenzo forgets to ever complain about, and overnight, he has started reading.

"He's still getting settled," Tano says. "Give him time."

As miserable as I feel, I suppose Tano is right. I need to give Lorenzo time. I need to give myself time. And as a member of the more mollycoddling Anglo culture, maybe what I really need is to look into assuming a more French attitude about the whole thing.

It would certainly be useful to compare notes with some of the other mothers, but thus far I have not found a way to break in, and Bonjourçava? is not working.

On any given Thursday or Friday, I sit on the steps of Célestins, quietly measuring my feminine existence against those of the James Bond girls and in particular the Charlie's Angels, with the fascination of a voyeur. None of them seem my natural soul mate, but the absence of close female friends is the glaring lacuna of my new life in Lyon and increasingly I yearn to absorb some modicum of the languorous insouciance they exude. Watching from the sidelines stirs up a visceral sense of long-ago first days at new schools and not feeling entirely cool enough. When I consider how I tried to convince Lorenzo of how easy it is to march up and insert yourself into a crowd of people that already know each other, I feel remiss.

But then, one fine Thursday a golden opportunity drops in my lap: The redhead needs to choose a new ringtone for her iPhone. I know this because I am, once again, eavesdropping on the three of them. They are sitting ahead of me on the steps, listening to clips of music and bantering about which song to choose.

"The Long and Winding Road." *Trop triste*—too sad.

"God Save the Queen." *Trop ard*, which means "trop hard," with a serious French accent.

"White Lines (Don't do it)." *Ouah! Parfait!*

Grandmaster Flash's groovster beat pours from a hot pink phone. My head nodding and my foot tapping, I am transported back to the Hôtel Ivoire, Abidjan, Ivory Coast. In the early eighties, every Friday afternoon, groups of us school kids went ice-skating at the luxury hotel that boasted the only rink (at the time, at least) in all of Africa. I smoked my first cigarettes at Hôtel Ivoire, made out with first boyfriends, and even choked back my first beer with my friends at the poolside bar.

Suddenly the hot pink phone rings, and my connection to the past disappears in thin air. Back at place des Célestins I realize, for the first time, that "White Lines," the song twelve-year-old me used to groove on down to, is actually about doing cocaine.

Apparently the Charlie's Angels still don't get it.

"*Le beat est funky,*" the blonde says, "but what does it mean?"

"*Excusez-moi,*" I say, leaning down toward them. "Do you need a translation?"

My insider understanding of Grandmaster Flash wins me instant approval and within minutes we are exchanging names. The bespectacled blonde is Bénédicte. She introduces me to Fanny, the hard-ass brunette, who has cut her hair into an even shorter pixie that accentuates her sharp cheekbones and light green eyes. Dominique is the redhead with the rocking new ring tone, and now that I have the chance to look her straight in the face, I see that she somehow resembles Arielle Dombasle, the actress cum singer cum Crazy Horse guest star who is married to BHL. (Lest you think BHL is some freakazoid rapper, those initials stand for Bernard-Henri Lévy. He is not a rapper, or a popstar, he is an "intellectual," a role which is revered in France.)

Béné. FanFan. Dom. These are the names they call each other. Once sensual holograms observed through an erotic scrim, now they are before me as real live conversation partners. We cover a few vital statistics—age (we're all forty-one), number of children (they each have just one), marital status (I am the only one of us who is married, although the Angels all have long term relationships with the fathers of their kids), and place of origin. Me, American transplant from Paris; the Angels, Lyonnaise to the core, all three born at Hôpital de la Croix-Rousse and raised right here in the Carré d'Or.

In fact, they have known each other since nursery school, and they all *went* to Lamartine.

My jaw drops.

This longevity of friendship is totally foreign to me. I have not a single friend who has known me all my life; if I go back through the yellow paged albums from pre-school and kindergarten, I have no idea of the destiny of 99 percent of the kids lined up next to me in those solemn class photos. The 1 percent I do know of are offered forth as snippets of gossip provided by neighborhood friends of my parents.

A joint circulates. (I was right! Although when Béné informs me this is the good stuff—*designer* weed, whatever that is—my jaw drops again.)

So the Angels went all the way through Lamartine together, and then attended the prestigious Catholic Ecole des Lazaristes, and then all three skipped University and went straight into sales of *produits de luxe*. Bénédicte once managed a fine china and crystal shop here in the Carré d'Or, whereas Dominique specialized in haute couture handbags and Fanny, shoes.

Now none of them work—they are all on *arrêt maladie*—which in France means a government-sanctioned medical leave. In other words, they do not ever report to a job, yet receive a steady income from the *sécurité sociale*. Why? Because they have all been diagnosed as *très fatigué*, which is really a semantic code for clinically depressed.

They ask me what I do, and without even thinking about it, I start to explain how I became a trailing wife and then couldn't find a job and *blah blah blah*. I stop myself right before I get to: "And then he had an affair and I left him…"

This is the part that women love to talk about. Lord knows that I know, for so many of my friendships in Paris are based on the sharing of our marital struggles, our dramas, what we have survived and how we deal with the men in our lives. Affairs are a particularly salient topic. I have even regretted sharing this information with certain friends, for they acted as though our marriage was permanently damaged; that there was no way a couple could ever recover, at least not without years of intensive psychotherapy.

Such stories don't just disappear from memory, not even with time, as my reaction to leaving Paris has proven. But the history is part of the background now, not part of the active scene. I realize, as this same old story rises up in my throat, ready to be regurgitated all over the steps of Célestins if only from rote memory of having recited it over so many years, that in Paris I have kept our identity as a couple predicated on our crisis. I clamp my mouth shut, just in time, realizing that it is no longer the story I want to define my marriage—or myself—by. It is passé, the narrative of ten years ago, and no longer a fair reflection of who we are as a couple—and who I am as a person.

Change your storyline, woman.

"I'm a psychotherapist. I had a fulltime practice in Paris until recently. Now I live in Lyon—because of my husband's job—and commute to Paris Mondays and Tuesdays."

I want to say more but my brief intro seems to be enough and with cursory nods they switch topics entirely: the reform of the school canteen. A study done by a secret parent's commission at the end of last school year revealed *fautes graves*, such as the fact that the children were being served *pamplemousse*—grapefruit— that was far too *acide*, and that the *veau au pruneaux* was not seasoned with enough panache.

Béné, FanFan, and Dom do not seem the type of mothers to join a secret canteen commission, but being French, talk of food quality is second nature to them. I keep to myself that over the years I, too, have sought out any opportunity to observe what the schools are feeding my kids, but this is because it usually looks so damn good I want to tap on the window of the cafeteria and ask the *dame de cantine* to send a doggy bag home for me.

The four of us look over the menu that Bénédicte picked up at school. Today the kids were served *green salad with balsamic vinaigrette with grilled chicken breast, scalloped potatoes, camembert, and apple compote.* Tomorrow the menu is *taboulé à la menthe, breaded fish filet served with ratatouille, brie, and a fresh fruit salad.*

Bof, the Angels say. This is the perfect French expression of insouciance and disregard. Again, I stay silent, because to my ears the canteen menu at Lamartine sounds nothing short of a Michelin-starred restaurant.

This idea I have, that my taste as an American must be somehow crude and callow compared to these stylish French women, however, is upended by their curiosity about where I shop for Lorenzo's clothes. They really like his *"look decontracté"*—as in, laid back—with those ripped-up jeans and scuffed up tennies with a big ol' hole in the toe.

Oh yeah, laid waaaaaay back, I say, dying with laughter inside my head. My son, the six-year-old trendsetter of the Carré d'Or. *Pourquoi pas?*

Twenty-Three

The next day I look for Bénédicte, Fanny, and Dominique at the gates of Ecole Lamartine, but somehow they manage to collect their sons and escape to Célestins before me. Maybe it is because I am moving slower than usual, teetering down the road in a pair of new high-heeled sandals that I bought that morning. *When in Rome and all,* I thought, and they felt comfortable when I tried them on in the store. Now the balls of my feet are throbbing and I have several raw blisters forming on my toes, but I push the pain from my mind when I spot the Angels, slouching on the steps of the theater, doling out *pains au lait* to their boys.

Still feeling rather saucy from the evening before, I *bise* them hello and take a place among them. We chat: clothes, hair, ringtones. Then I produce the treat I bought at Pignol, a gaily ribboned pack of *guimauve*, otherwise known as *chamallow*— marshmallow—to share with my new friends.

Now, if the word "marshmallow" conjures an image of jet-puffed jumbo mallows, the kind that American summer camps buy in bulk for sticky-faced kids to shove on sticks and set flame to over the campfire, this may sound like a strange choice to woo my new gal pals with.

Rien à voir.

These chamallow, handmade at Pignol, are nothing short of biting into an edible cloud. With just the faintest fraction of a millimeter of a crusty sugar coat, and an inside that is so soft, so chewy but airy, fresh guimauve, sliced into these wonderful spongy cubes, is one of those things (at least for those of us raised on Jet Puffs) that makes you say—and in the best way—*only in France.*

But all three Angels decline as I wave the packet before them: *Non, merci.*

I might have suspected that for women who grew up with Pignol, a sachet of gourmet marshmallow would not entice them.

Still, I say, opening the packet, "Are you sure?"

"*Je ne veux pas terminer tout enveloppée,*" Bénédicte answers, lighting a cigarette.

I giggle, a little embarrassed. That she doesn't want to end up "all enveloped" is a euphemism for *fat.*

I was first warned about getting *enveloppé*ed when I was pregnant with Lorenzo. My gynecologist, a no-nonsense, stick-thin mother of four who had no sympathy for my unbearable hunger, harped at me every single pre-natal visit that I was gaining far too much weight and was going to end up "enveloped."

Given that I tower over the Charlie's Angels by at least six inches, and outweigh each of them by at least forty pounds, I might have gleaned that snarfing down a bag of marshmallows mid-afternoon was not part of their stay-stick-thin diet plan.

I rattle the bag once more, but by then all three of them have cigarettes in hand, and so while they puff, I get enveloped. I am debating whether I will look like a total pig if I gobble down the whole bag, but before I can decide, another beautiful woman that I have noticed in the James Bond crowd lunges at me for a kiss.

Mwah mwah. Our lips pucker the air by each other's cheeks.

I blush. I have always disliked this tradition of kissing someone I have just met, but before I can even process who I have planted my smacker on, Fanny introduces me as *"une Anglaise-Parisienne."*

An English-Parisian?

Now there's an identity. I even kind of like it, except, of course, for the fact that I am *not* English, and my insider knowledge of Grandmaster Flash did not seem to drive that point home.

"Nice, nice," the woman says, in English, in a strangely clipped accent that makes it sound like she's saying *niece.* "I have did my studies in *Londres* when I am young girl. You are from *Londres?"*

"In fact, I am *américaine,"* I start to say, but then Lorenzo runs up to ask if he can have one of those gorgeous marshmallows. But he knows by now that marshmallows like this have exotic flavors—*rose, fleur d'oranger, pistache...* and he only likes the *vanille* ones.

The woman studies us with interest as we have this quick little exchange in English, all questions of whether I am a transplant from London forgotten—by her. On my side, I have privately decided that if she wants to think I am from London, she can go right ahead. It would not be the first time I pretend, by omission, to be from somewhere else.

One time I was standing in line at Paris's most famous department store, BHV—the Bazaar de l'Hôtel de Ville—Carmen, Lorenzo, and Matthew in tow. Carmen and Matthew must have been about eight and six, and Lorenzo was a toddler. The line dragged on and on, and right before it was my turn to pay, Lorenzo wobbled off toward a stack of books on display. I turned for a second to reel him back to my side, and in that moment, a haughty high-heeled woman pushed past me and stole my turn at the register.

Perhaps she assumed that, clearly foreign, I would cower before her churlish bad manners and just let her butt in line. But she did not know that I had been in Paris for at least six years by then, and that I was *way* beyond putting up with this kind of bullshit.

"I cannot believe how rude you are!" I said, pushing back in front of her, blood pounding through my veins. "What is wrong with you? Especially when you can see that I'm here with three young children!"

Our voices escalated until we were both shouting. I never behaved this way in public and was aware, as this terrible verbal brawl was unfurling, that my venomous attitude was that of a woman who was done being taken advantage of because she was an outsider. When the surrounding customers grew impatient they expressed being on my side, and the boorish woman finally abandoned her purchases and flounced out of the store shouting, "Go back to England where you belong!"

I was almost blinded by the adrenaline pumping through me, and shame at this ugly public altercation, and fumbled to pay quickly and get out of there.

Then, through my dismay, I heard Carmen's voice. "You're *so* brave, Mom."

"And she thought you were *English!*" Matthew said.

The kids just thought that was hilarious.

You? English?

Ha!Ha!Ha!

Back at Célestins, the woman who thinks I am a Londoner tousles Lorenzo's hair. "*Eees your son?*"

"Yes, he's six."

"*SIX ANS?*" She sounds totally shocked. "*Mais il est IMMENSE! ENORME!*"

He's huge! Enormous!

Lorenzo stands there looking uncomfortable, although this sort of commentary is nothing new. I dig a vanilla cube from the sachet and hand it to him, swallowing my irritation. How many times in the last ten years have I had to listen to someone shriek on about the utter *hugeness* of my kids—and right in front of them!

I find it stunningly rude.

I fantasize, sometimes, of responding with something equally impolite, like, "And *your* kid is a shrimp. Why is he so *scrawny?*"

But it is not in my nature to attack this way, although the mama bear instinct comes out in full force when I think someone is hurting one of my children. And I have no doubt that such commentaries do hurt, for Carmen has asked me many times over the years, always sounding wholly disconsolate, "Why am I so *big* compared to all the French kids?"

"Look at their *parents*, honey," I always reply, trying to draw attention to the fact that for my five feet eight inches and Tano's six feet three inches, most of the parents of her French counterparts are considerably shorter.

"Short parents, short kids, tall parents, tall kids," I tell her. "And tall is fabulous," I add, wanting to boost her up.

"Then why do people make it sound like there's something *wrong* with me?" Carmen usually answers.

From the look on Lorenzo's face right now, it seems that this very question has just materialized in his brain. My tall, sweet boy. I feel like clocking that woman. But she has already moved on down the line of people to kiss on the steps of Célestins and so instead I turn back to Fanny.

"Ummm, Fanny, I'm *American*, not English."

But just then Jean-Claude pelts the soccer ball toward the boys he is playing with, yet his aim is off by a good three meters and the ball flies straight at his mother.

"*J'en ai marre!*" She screams, flying off the steps and flogging his arm with her purse. "*T'es nul!*"

France has recently been touted as some sort of developmental mecca for children, largely because of books written by Americans about the superior parenting skills of French parents. This is a cultural myth as far as I am concerned, for there is as much parental screaming here as there is anywhere else in the world. (And loads of bratty kids, too.)

FanFan's admonishment of Jean-Claude seems unnecessarily cruel—it was an accident, for God's sake—although maybe it all sounds worse to my ears because it's in French. In any case, the clarification of where I hail from disappears in the scuffle.

I feel a bit miffed, but also a bit high maintenance—*does it really matter?* After all, I am accustomed to forging relationships with people who will never make it to my side of the world. That is the very nature of the expat's life: It is divided, compartmental-ized across geographic boundaries and into cultural and linguis-tic spheres. There is the crowd that you belong to in your place of expatriation, in which the people you enter into relationships with will likely never visit your specific place of origin, and then there are all the people from your specific place of origin who will never know the places you make home.

My mind flashes to the story of my sister Steph, who, her first year of college, couldn't find a comfortable way to keep re-explain-ing her complicated geographic trajectory when she landed in a dorm of people who had grown up together in eastern Maryland.

So she finally started telling everyone she was from California.

At the time I thought this was so weird, so maladaptive… and now, all these years later, I suddenly understand. Although I won't go so far as to say I am English, it really is so much simpler to just be an Anglo from Paris, to cancel out any detail of what came prior to that, the story behind Paris, of my nomadic child-hood, my bicultural marriage, our Argentinean-Italian-American kids who know only France as home…

It all seems so complicated, so chaotic and snarled, why offer an explanation if no one asks?

I could say I am from anywhere, really.

Who will follow up?

Twenty-Four

One Thursday evening when I roll home spacey-eyed after another session on the steps of Célestins, Tano says, "Are you *stoned?*"

I explain the situation in the way I have rationalized it: Thursday and Friday afternoons are like a protracted cultural immersion program. My relationship to the Charlie's Angels has made me realize, among other things, just how insulated my Parisian life really was. In Paris, most of my close friends were foreign working girls, preoccupied with making a living, like me. So these end of the week joint-and-gab-fests feel justified: I am learning all about *French* culture.

"Excuse me," Tano says. "It is not 'French culture' you are learning about. It is the culture of the *haute bourgeoisie.*"

The upper class. Which, of course, deep down, I know.

And I also know Tano is right when he says, "I seriously hope that you're not going to start smoking again."

"Cigarettes or weed?" I ask, although even as the words leave my mouth I know it is a ridiculous question. The man is a doctor, for Pete's sake.

He shoots me a withering look. "When are you going to get serious about starting your professional life here in Lyon?"

This is a sore subject, although I suppose I have brought these questions on myself, as I am unable to keep it quiet every time I get a phone call—average one per week—from someone looking for an English-speaking therapist in Lyon.

How they get my number is no mystery—I put my name on a France-wide, English-speaking therapists directory and thus far, for the Rhône-Alpes region, I am the only native English speaker offering therapy services. I never expected to get so many calls, though, and have been totally unprepared for them, namely because I don't have an office.

Tano thinks I should transform our living room into a work space, as I did when I started working in Paris ten years earlier, and that I should be spending time on building up a referral base. This, however, would require doing all sorts of networking that I cannot imagine trying to fit in on Thursdays and Fridays (least of all when there is the housework and the cultural immersion program with the Charlie's Angels to consider).

The whole discussion leads me back to this indelible image I have of my mother, stretched out on the sofa after work, sipping a Diet Coke and stealing a moment for herself. (The country, house, and sofa of this memory often change, but the image of my mother in this posture, Diet Coke in hand, remains consistent.)

"I don't know why women fought for the right to work," she'd say. "To me it's the worst oppression there is."

A little giggle escapes my lips.

"You think it's funny," Tano says, misinterpreting the source of my laughter. "But we agreed that you would start transferring your professional life to Lyon."

"Yes," I say, my voice rising, "but I need an OFFICE before I can start working."

"Then do something about it!" he snaps.

It's not so easy to just set up a practice, I almost bark back. But truthfully, the fact that Tano almost never raises his voice is the very reason I recount his irritation here, for it is a mark of the concern (and disdain) he must feel, seeing me breeze home with bloodshot eyes, no trace of my usual go-getting attitude in sight.

How to reveal to him that part of me is secretly grateful that I haven't found an office? Irrational though it may be, if in Paris I know exactly how to be an effective therapist, in Lyon I feel like an impostor. Several months in, I already feel entrenched in two distinct personas: the Paris me and the Lyon me. The Paris me feels solid—professional and full of purpose—taking the train with my little black carry-on, sitting in my beloved office and helping people chisel away at their personal conundrums. The Lyon me plays homemaker and stay-at-home mom, but self medicates with joints and regresses back to that insecure mode of feeling that what I look like is as important—if not more important—than what I do.

And the deeper I delve into this Lyon persona, the more incompetent I feel. How will I ever pull a whole new practice together down here? Every week I am losing more confidence, and the fact that this move has proven to be so stressful only compounds the idea. If I was worth my weight wouldn't I have found a more appropriate apartment for us? Wouldn't Lorenzo be happier? Wouldn't I be saying "no" to joints instead of taking big old puffs the minute they're passed my way?

Conveniently, Béné's dealer is arrested, and so the Thursday-Friday apathy sticks grind to an immediate halt the following week. Now on the steps of Célestins, the Angels chain smoke Gitanes, and I turn back to snarfing down Lorenzo's goûter.

"*Tu vas perdre ton ligne,*" Fanny warns. You'll lose your figure.

"*Bof,*" I answer, although her assessment sends a jolt of anxiety through my body.

Béné and Dom laugh, but Fanny won't let me off the hook that easily. "*Mais pourquoi tu n'es pas plus inspiré avec ton look?*"

Why don't I take better care of my appearance?

I freeze mid-chew, feeling the blood creep up my neck into my cheeks.

She musses my hair, pulled back in a messy bun. "*Pourquoi tu ne te fais jamais un brushing?*"

A brushing is my most despised hair-related activity, in which the hair dresser is paid to turn one's locks into a highly "done" style, usually requiring lots of hot blow drying and copious squirts of hairspray.

Then she fingers my favorite old green sweater. "*Tu ne te mets pas en valeur.*"

Mettre en valeur: to enhance, promote, play up. The term is euphemistic, and can be applied to different things, but in the case of feminine image, which happens to be the case in which I most often hear it used, it pertains to making the most of what you've got. Not, "if you've got it, flaunt it," but more, "whatever you've got, make it better—and *then* flaunt it."

Fanny points to my comfy pink tennies. "*Pourquoi tu ne portes jamais des talons?*"

Why don't you ever wear heels?

What is this—Head, Shoulders, Knees, and Toes? I think. If she yanked off my shoes she'd see that my feet are in a state of emergency after the few weeks that I tottered around in those awful high sandals.

"Leave her alone, Fanny," Béné says. "She doesn't play the game."

I am grateful that Béné has jumped in on my behalf, although the analysis she offers—that I don't play the game, of femininity, of seduction—makes me feel exposed and ashamed.

"It just makes me uncomfortable," I try to explain, although I am aware of how completely weird I must sound.

"Although it is strange," Béné adds, not unkindly. "We become invisible as we age. Why would a woman do that to herself on purpose?"

Now I feel a little hurt. I may not have been making huge efforts with my external image, but I wouldn't say I had disappeared completely.

"Think how your appearance will affect Carmen," Béné goes on.

The sound of my daughter's name makes me instantly defensive. The universal cult of female appearance is so visible here in France where my lovely, smart girl is coming of age, surrounded at every turn by the naked and perfectly airbrushed behinds and breasts that adorn the sides of news kiosks, pharmacy windows, and billboards. I want nothing more than to protect her from the obsession with appearance, knowing too well how it leads to estrangement from self.

I decide to share a little story from my mid-twenties, when my hairdresser talked me into cutting my long hair into a swingy, shoulder length bob. Jodie Foster wore her hair that way that season and apparently it was all the rage.

Snip-snip. Off came the hair and God, I loved it! It felt fantastic and light and sporty. *I* felt fantastic and light and sporty. I drove to the Youth Center where I worked at that time, and when I walked into the main room where ten street kids lounged around in various states of repose, the supervisor in charge, this big beer-bellied tattooed social worker named Chuck, took one look and shouted, "Why'd ya cut your hair? You don't look NEARLY as sexy anymore."

Too humiliated to consider that maybe the real issue was not my hair but the rude, inappropriate attitude of that slob Chuck, I crumpled. I wanted to die: of embarrassment, shame, and fear. Yes, fear—that I really was no longer sexy and appealing and if I lost that then who the fuck was I? And now the hair was gone! It was as though I had been stripped bare in public.

As I stood there having an internal meltdown, one of the other staff people at the Youth Center, this utter gem of a woman, shot back: "Is it her fucking job to look SEXY, Chuck? HUH?"

The Angels listen to my story with these expressions on their faces that say: *That's fascinating but <u>why</u> are you telling us this?* Then Dominique says, "Women get *power* from their appearance. You do realize that, don't you?"

In that moment I see that my fascination with the Charlie's Angels is not because of how different we are, but how alike. I suddenly understand that all of their discussions about makeup and clothes and seduction are actually just a subtext for power.

For control.

They cling to their images as perfectly groomed sex kittens the way I once did, and the way that I now cling to this idea of myself as an independent Parisian career woman.

"You should see Dr. Barnie," Béné says.

"Who's that?"

"*Mon psy... behn, notre psy,*" she says, gesturing to Fanny and Dom who are now listening in and nodding their agreement.

Psy is short for psychiatrist, or psychologist, but given that this is France, whether one or the other, the psy in question is undoubtedly a Freudian.

"He can help you with this complex."

"You may need medication—"

"Maybe hypnosis..."

"Or at least psychoanalysis."

Somehow I am not enticed by the idea of Dr. Barnie, who I can only visualize as a big purple dinosaur in a beret. He sees all three of the Angels? I can't help but find that suspicious, especially when you consider that all three of them have been deemed *trop malade*—too sick—to return to the working world.

Is it Dr. Barnie who manipulates the system?

Or have the Angels manipulated him to keep them signed off as unwell?

Abuse of the social security system is a hot topic here in France. You hear about it in the news all the time, yet it is not a subject that remains distant, one that you hear about but don't personally know anyone implicated. I know many French people who cheat the system as though it's not only second nature, but a God-given right.

One friend boasted how his doctor had put him on arrêt maladie for a "sore arm" so that he could have an extra two weeks at home after his daughter was born.

Another friend was put on arrêt for—nudge nudge, wink wink, as she tells it—fatigue.

And of the pregnant women I have known in my thirteen years in France *all* of them ended up on arrêt for the duration of their pregnancy, from five months or so, because of "cramps." (Cramps being what in Anglo culture is commonly accepted as the innocuous Braxton Hicks "practice" contractions.) When I was pregnant with Lorenzo every French mother I knew suggested coming down with "cramps" so I could be put on arrêt.

I was sorely tempted—getting paid and not having to work sounded fabulous. But when I inquired at the bureau that represents self-employed people, the answer was, "You don't work you don't get paid." Then, even more so than now, it was unthinkable for me to give up my financial stability.

And so I kept working.

Back on the steps of Célestins I reach for another cookie. Someone has bought a pack of *Petit Ecoliers* for the kids—a buttery biscuit with a square of milk chocolate in the middle—and I am having a hard time controlling myself.

"*Tu es vraiment <u>très</u> gourmande*," Béné concedes.

What this means, in literal terms, is that I have a sweet tooth, but what I suspect it really means, coming from this perfectly in-control twigster, is "you are a big fat pig."

"Okay, okay," I say, eager to change the subject. "Give me Dr. Barnie's number. Maybe I'll go see him."

But the Charlie's Angels have my *relooking* on their mind. They begin a serious disquisition on the dry skin of my cheeks, the redness of my nose, my messy hair, my untweezed brows...

"Oui," Dominique concludes, studying my face. "You really should do your eyebrows. If you just shaped them a little here, trimmed them a little there..."

I close my eyes as her cool fingers tap lightly at my brow.

"Next time you go for *ton épilation...*"

Epilation is waxing, and while this is certainly not an exclusively French practice (there's a reason it's called the Brazilian), it is undoubtedly much more popular here than anywhere else I've lived. I know many American women who have stuck with the painless and antiquated razor for hair removal, and who consider hair removal to be a duty only up to the knee and in the armpit... and maybe not at all in winter. Then there are the women who don't believe in hair removal at all, who let their armpits and legs get as hairy as nature made them.

This diversity of personal hair removal habits *must* also exist in France. Not that I have ever met a French woman without her own personal *esthéticienne* for the extensive removal of body hair, and I don't just mean legs and 'pits.

Still, I am not prepared for the reaction when I confess that I never do my eyebrows when I do my épilation, because I never do l'épilation.

"*QUOI? TU N'EPILES PAS?*"

I shrug with what I hope looks like my own breed of mystery. The truth is I just cannot imagine letting someone poor hot wax on my crotch. Jesus. I was not even able to complete my "pelvic re-education" after giving birth to Lorenzo. (For the unfamiliar: every woman who gives birth in France is entitled to see a physical therapist who will kindly provide low grade electric shock therapy to the vagina to get those pelvic muscles zapped back into shape. The cost of this treatment is actually covered by the social security system.)

But the Angels *have* to know: If I don't epilate how does my husband cope with *le cunnilingus?*

I gape at the discovery that their men are apparently doing le cunnilingus to them all the time.

Béné, FanFan, Dom.... Their lives seem so sexy—unbridled, really—while mine, comparatively, seems wholesome, G-rated, *boring.*

Yet, paradoxically, my life also seems out of control compared to theirs that are just so ordered.

Ordered sexiness, that's it: two things I never really thought went together but that I know now, from the Angels' stories, seems to be an essential component to their identities as sensual women in their forties. Like the way they strictly regulate mealtime, bedtime, playtime and clean-up time for their children, sex time is a "protocol," like any other. Béné and her long-term boyfriend Jean-Sylvestre do "it" every other day, she reveals, never the same position twice in the same week, plus a weekly blow job.

Oh la la, Fanny argues. *Every two days? Le protocole* is important but *quand même.* She is on an every-three-day schedule, which has Dominique, who does it daily without fail, laughing (although she concedes that this is due in part to the fact that her boyfriend is ten years younger than she is. A man as old as my husband probably wouldn't want le protocole that frequently... Would he?).

I have no idea. But, I explain priggishly, I am far too exhausted to find out.

Forget about fatigue, they coach. Le protocole is *une responsabilité.*

"No, really," I insist.

"*Une petite fellation, alors!*" Then just give him a blow job!

Pride leads me to play along that I will become the blow job queen of rue du Président Edouard Herriot, although inside I wonder if I am the only woman in the world who finds une petite fellation far more exhausting than just having a quickie.

They are determined to help me operationalize this. "*Alors,* what time do the kids go to bed?"

"9:30."

"*Bon.* At 9:45 you should be down on your knees..."

Apparently in their households "bedtime" is not followed by a series of "MOOOOOOOOOOOMs!"

"Honestly, *les filles,*" I say. "I am *très fatiguée* by that time of day..."

"You don't *let* yourself be tired. You wake yourself up with *le petit vibro* before dinner."

Le petit vibro is French for little vibrator. They don't give me time to ask if I am supposed to be wielding my sex toy in front of my children while we do homework. Because the next suggestion involves *des oeufs*—eggs—vibrating eggs, that is.

"You can keep one in your *culotte,*" Béné says, "and your husband can control the speed by *télécommande* while you cook dinner."

This scenario strikes me as absurdly funny, and I sprawl back on the steps of Célestins and laugh. Yet the Charlie's Angels are not laughing with me.

"It's not a joke," Dominique says. "*Les jeux de seduction sont importants.*"

Seduction games are important, eh? I think to myself, as I take note of their circumspect glances. Clearly they think I am a serious case. Something is definitely out of balance in my life, their looks say, if I am too exhausted to play les jeux de seduction, too wound up with my kids to perform une petite fellation.

I don't really want to admit it to myself, but part of me thinks they must be right.

Mon Dieu.

Twenty-Five

That night in bed I grab a fistful of my thighs, feeling the rough little hairs sprouting out in a messy pattern. My thoughts drift to the Charlie's Angels, their sensual femininity, their smooth, hairless legs, and some distant fantasy about other hairless parts of their bodies. Then I start thinking about how women in Argentina wax, too. How have I been married to a South American man all these years and never considered that maybe he finds my pubic hair repulsive?

Feeling like a shaggy gorilla, I whisper Tano's name.

"Mmmmm?" he mutters, half asleep.

Protected by the dark, I divulge my new insecurity.

"Oh please," he mutters, in a tone that tells me he doesn't care to discuss this any further. "It's female genital mutilation."

"You think?" I say hopefully, although my mind is already racing over the arguments that could be made against this laconic statement. *Is toenail cutting a form of mutilation? Hair cutting?*

I have trouble sleeping as my mind is preoccupied with this question—to wax or not to wax?—and God, I *do* know it is ridiculous, but these communications with the Angels have made me realize just how far I have strayed from what women are "supposed" to do. In fact, the "new" marriage model of frequent, ahem–*contact* – is now so much the old model, I cannot even remember the last time we did it.

The next morning I feel headachey and sore-throaty, and am only half-listening when Carmen announces that she wants to quit guitar.

"*Qué?*" Tano says. "*Porqué?*"

"I just don't think I'll ever be really good at it," she says. "Not like you, Pop. And I don't feel like spending so much time on it when I have so many other things to do."

"Well you can't just quit," I say, thinking of all the cajoling I had to do to get her a spot at this particular music studio, not to mention the fact that I had to pay in advance for all the lessons.

"Why not? You did."

"What did I quit?" My crabby tone betrays that I have barely had my first sip of coffee.

"You quit organizing your new life down here."

"What on earth are you talking about?" I am suddenly fully awake.

Carmen is a tough cookie and looks squarely at me, saying: "A looong time ago you said you were going to start your private practice in Lyon so that you wouldn't have to keep leaving us, and you haven't done anything about it."

"*Haven't done anything about it?*" I practically shriek. "Have you seen how busy I am trying to keep everything together for EVERYONE?"

I am aware that my reaction is disproportionate, but God, it's just so unfair to be confronted—and first thing in the morning, too—about something that would be cliché if it were not so real: the struggle to balance career and family.

I turn to Tano for reinforcement but he shrugs and says, "You always have one foot out the door."

How has everything gotten so convoluted? Is there no recognition at all that a woman might have legitimate reasons to maintain her independence? Somewhere along the way I know I that I have made allusions to getting myself sorted in Lyon, but between Tano and Carmen you'd think I had broken some sort of contract.

Still, Carmen's comment feels like a punch in the stomach. This is how my daughter sees me? All talk, no action, and someone who keeps leaving her because of it.

The minute Tano and the kids leave, I sit in front of the computer feeling overwhelmed. My office search thus far has only revealed that the *cabinets* offered by real estate agencies are way too big and way too expensive. My next plan is to do a mailing—fifty letters to fifty different therapists within a two-kilometer radius of our apartment, asking if anyone has a space to sublet—but I need someone to help me with the French and there just never seems to be a calm moment. By mid-morning though, my throat is so raw I call Tano.

"Do a salt water gargle," he says. "Or look in one of my travel kits. I think there might be some lozenges in one of them."

Per Tano's orders, I gargle, relieved to have an excuse to abandon the office search. Then I go to his closet where he has an assortment of little overnight toiletries bags, of the variety they distribute on night flights, big enough for a small toothbrush, socks, and a mask to cover the eyes. I start opening them in search of throat lozenges and find aspirin, anti-malarials, and *CONDOMS?*

It is a strip of six and though they have that aspect of having kicked around for some time in a bag with razors and toothpaste tubes, my heart pounds with adrenaline.

Why the hell does he have condoms?

We certainly hadn't used them any time recently, nor during that fabulous chapter of the new marriage model (which had led to more than one fright around late periods -- still somehow worth it because the spontaneity has been so *reviving*).

Stay calm, I tell myself. Finding some condoms does not mean anything about my marriage. But I can't stop my thoughts from racing back to the discovery of Estelle, to forcing Tano to get an HIV test even though he assured me *they* had always used protection, to me telling him, when I took him back, "If you EVER cheat on me again you BETTER WEAR A CONDOM!"

Oh my God, had he taken that as an invitation?

Lozenges forgotten, I race to the phone, condoms in hand, and dial Tano's number.

He answers on the second ring. "I'm in a meeting," he whispers. "Can I call you back?"

All that I manage to answer comes out as a strange sniffling sob. I hear Tano say "*Excusez-moi, il y a une urgence,*" and over the sound of his chair pushing back and his footsteps on the floor of some distant meeting room he says, "Are you okay? Are the kids okay?"

"I found your condoms," I cry.

"*What?*"

"Your *condoms*. They were with the throat lozenges."

"I have no idea what you are talking about." He sounds truly puzzled but also truly annoyed. "And I am extremely busy. Can this wait until tonight?"

I hesitate. Waiting until tonight will give him the rest of the day to come up with any number of excuses for what those condoms are doing in his toiletries kit, although it occurs to me, in some distant corner of my mind, that given that he sent me straight to the hiding place of the contraband material, there may be a legitimate reason he has them.

We get off the phone, agreeing that he'll try to come home early, and with nothing else to do than wait, I turn back to the task of scrolling through the addresses of therapists in the near vicinity. The dissonance between my current dilemma—how to find an office—and this much larger issue—can I trust my husband?—is too much, though, and I finally just lie down on the sofa, office project abandoned.

I am aware of how my mind is drawn to worst-case-scenario: *Condoms equals he must be cheating on me and how could I have been so dumb to follow him down here?*

Thing is, unlike when I discovered the affair with Estelle, and all those cracks in our shared existence suddenly made sense, I cannot think of a single gap between us now. Back in East Africa when his affair took place, Tano and I were deeply disconnected from each other. We were no longer sharing the details of our respective lives, no longer chatting amiably about the banal and reflectively about the important. We barely knew each other at that time and preferred it that way for we really had stopped even liking each other, either.

Could I say the same now?

Hardly. We shared *everything*: the big, the small, the silly, the frustrating. We kept in touch and looked out for each other and reveled in our children together. We were actually really, truly a happy family.

So much so that I actually cannot believe that he could be cheating on me. He couldn't. He *wouldn't*.

But what about those condoms?

Twenty-Six

That afternoon I am back on the steps of place des Célestins with the Charlie's Angels. I feel morose but I hide it, not ready to divulge this long and complicated history. In spite of my angst about the discussion Tano and I will have tonight, I feel protective of my marriage, and defensive, too. Who knows what the Angels would think about Tano if I were to reveal the discovery of the condoms. No longer did I need the women in my life to commiserate about what jerks men are, but I also couldn't bear to listen to the "men will be men" rationale. Nor did I want this story to become the proof that my unwillingness to take le protocole seriously has led to an infraction, if that's what I face.

In other words, I don't really want to share my fears with the Angels' because I don't yet feel safe with them.

Lest that sound snooty, let it be stated for the record I am grateful to have cobbled together this group of girlfriends, even if the relationships are still not completely easy. First of all, even though we spend most Thursday and Friday afternoons together, the Charlie's Angels never wait for me at the school gates, as they wait for each other, to walk to Célestins together. I am not so immature that I actually care that Lorenzo and I have to travel the twenty meters by ourselves. But I gather they miss the time when it was just the three of them, and I hate the idea that I am intruding on their private time with each other. And I know that there is a deeper, private side to their lives as I have been exposed to snippets of it in fits and starts, in references they make to each other in my company without ever providing the background: the death of Béné's sister when they were teenagers, Dom's past addiction to cocaine, Fanny's struggles with money management. From the allusions they make to the hypnotist they periodically consult to help with their willpower to stop eating, it seems that all three also share some history of disordered eating that is not fully under control. I cringe when I think about how I waved that bag of fancy marshmallows at them.

The women are the women and the boys are the boys, though, so most Friday evenings I invite their sons to come play with Lorenzo sometime over the weekend, but they always decline, reporting plans with extended family. I get it—if my family were anywhere nearby I'd be meeting up with them, as well. But the Angels are not careful with the remarks they make, and often when I sit with them the following week, details of the hilarious moments they shared the weekend before slip out.

I suspect that the Charlie's Angels think I am not sufficiently "*cadré*"—structured—with Lorenzo, and that is why they don't want to release their kids to my care for a simple play date. They have already told me that they think it is problematic that I let Lorenzo eat as much goûter as he wants, not to mention the fact that I don't reprimand his sloppy handwriting. Then there was that homework assignment about the letter *D*. The boys were to read a short paragraph, complete with illustrations, called *La Dame et La Robe*. The *Dame* has a very large *Derrière*, so big in fact that it *Déchirés* (tears) the fabric of her dress, revealing her backside. Her boyfriend *David* laughs and she smacks his face.

Seriously?

This little ditty would never make it into an Anglo reading lesson for six year olds! I tried to explain my amusement to the Angels, but our cultural baselines are so distinct that all the humor dissolved like an effervescent tablet when I started explaining how in the United States we wouldn't consider it appropriate to call attention to someone's backside, especially not a woman's because of female objectification, and *blah blah blah*.

Ah, bon?

This is the thing about being foreign: You never know for sure if you are breaking some subtle rules of comportment which hold enough power to make you seem untrustworthy, or ridiculous, or bizarre.

And this circles back to the reason I don't want to discuss the condoms. What if the Angels think something untoward about me? That I am to blame? That I am a drama queen? A pushover? A prude?

Since I don't know what to think myself, I am not ready to work it out *en groupe*. But as it turns out, I am saved from having to make a decision about whether to tell them because of the identical note that we and all the other mothers scattered around Célestins find in our children's book bags: The school is going on strike, every Tuesday, for the next three weeks.

As mentioned earlier, I am accustomed to all the strikes that take place in France, including the ones that close down schools for days at a time.

But Tuesday is one of my days in Paris.

And I don't live on a kibbutz anymore.

What am I going to do with Lorenzo?

MERDE.

The Angels are not bothered by the strike. They will scatter to the nearby suburbs—Oullins, Ecully, Craponne (if the French only knew how unfortunate that name is to Anglo ears)—where their parents have moved in their retirement.

I muster every drop of my brainpower to send a telepathic message: *Please invite Lorenzo to join you, please invite Lorenzo.*

But none of them extends the invitation. And then, as anxiety churns in my stomach—*what am I going to do? Ask Tano to stay home from work? Miss one day of a two-day work week every day for the next three weeks? Look for a babysitter?*—Dominique says, "*Oui, les grèves sont vraiment chiantes.*" Strikes suck.

I don't mean to sound petulant, because I know that the Charlie's Angels have no obligation to me or my son, but all I want to do is shout: *Stop complaining! Your lives are easy! You have family nearby!*

Of course I bite my tongue. But in moments like these I literally yearn for the Oberkampf kibbutz. The school strikes are nationwide and already I can imagine the information exchange taking place in our old building: the kids psyched to have days off and the parents deciding who will be in charge of lunch on a given Tuesday.

Even though I know it is not fair to me, the mother (will Tano beat himself up over this same question?), I feel like a shitty mom for thinking about my work, not my kid, at the news of the strike. I feel totally shitty knowing that if I manage to organize it, I will not be available when the strike occurs, because I *will* be back at work.

I have been separating from Paris slowly but surely, but today, with the condoms and now the news of the strike, I miss my old life like crazy. It is almost more than I can bear.

That evening Tano does not get home early; he gets home late because there is some complication at work that has kept him in meetings all day long. Whereas I have been preparing to answer to the questions I am sure he will ask as soon as he bounds through the door—*Darling, what happened? What condoms? And how are you feeling as I can imagine how this has upset you!*—instead, I have to remind him we even have something to discuss.

"Oh yeah," he says, thumbing through the mail. "What is that all about?"

I beckon for him to follow me to the bedroom, where the condoms are now hidden under my pillow. I pull them out and dangle them before him.

"I found these."

"So?"

"What do you mean, 'so'?"

"I mean, so what? I don't understand what the problem is."

This conversation is not going the way I imagined, nor is Tano acting like a guy caught in the act and trying to cover his tracks.

"Why do *you* have condoms?"

"Because at one moment in time I had hope that you might agree to have sex with me from time to time."

He says this casually, no sarcasm whatsoever. Then he tears open one of the envelopes and starts reading some form letter from the bank.

"We have sex from time to time!"

"Oh, really?" he says. "In any event, I bought those condoms a few years ago, when you kept saying that you were afraid of getting pregnant again."

"That was when Lorenzo was still a baby—"

"And when he was a toddler, and when he was four, and *now*—"

"Hey!"

He tears open another envelope. "Why are you so concerned anyway?"

"After everything we've been through?! If you have condoms, it's for a *reason*."

"Well I told you the *actual* reason. But if I did have those condoms for the reason I know you are thinking of, wouldn't that at least be appropriate?"

I feel my face getting hot. *Don't start crying*, I hiss inside my head, but the tears spill freely. They are tears of relief, because I believe what he is saying to me. I needn't have been so worried. But will it ever go away completely, this sense that betrayal is just an inch away?

"*Kreestin*," he says, putting his arms around me. "If I had wanted to have affairs would I have begged you to come live with me in Lyon?"

He has a point, and a small laugh escapes me. "But can you see my point? What would you have thought if you found condoms in *my* bag?"

"Honestly, I don't know... but I do know that I can't control you."

"Meaning *I* can't control *you*."

"Meaning we can't control each other. I don't *want* to control you anymore than I want to feel that you are controlling me. We're not in this as police."

We stare at each other for a long moment. Then he says, "I guess if I found condoms in your bag I would stop and wonder. But what I would think about is what matters to me more than anything else: if you love *me*. How you treat *me*."

Suddenly Lorenzo appears. "I'm hungry, Mom."

I tell him to skedaddle and wash his hands; that I'll be right there to organize dinner. I just have one last thing to ask. "And do you feel that I love you?"

"I do," he says. "Although if I had to measure that by the number of times in a month..."

I swat at him as he waves the condoms at me. I am about to say something sassy like, "You know I've been reading up on these Lyonnais protocols..." but then I hear: "MOOOOOOOOOM!"

I press myself into Tano's arms and give him a slow kiss right on the lips. His beard tickles my face.

"MOOOOOOOOOM!"

"That screaming," I say, "such an aphrodisiac." I step away from Tano, visions of an uninspired pasta dish already dancing through my head. Maybe those vibrating eggs would work to spice up the daily dinner slog.

As I leave the room Tano says, "Don't worry about the condoms. They will keep for another six years."

Twenty-Seven

In the end, I needn't have gotten so stressed out about the strikes. For the next three Tuesdays, Tano takes Lorenzo to work with him. Lorenzo is thrilled. He gets to sit in Pop's office and play Carmen's old Nintendo game, and when he tires of that, Tano gives him fifty-centime pieces to feed into the snack machine down the hall. They have pizza one lunch time, steak and fries another, and the third Tuesday, Lorenzo gets to attend the office-wide catered luncheon to say good-bye to some departing colleagues.

Evenings they wander over to the official store of Olympique Lyonnais, Lyon's beloved soccer team, where Lorenzo ogles the posters and jerseys, and Tano, a total and complete softie when it comes to anything related to his kids or soccer, buys Lorenzo all the paraphernalia his little heart desires.

The last Tuesday of the strike, when I am finally back in Lyon, we stand arm in arm in the darkness of Lorenzo's bedroom. He is sleeping peacefully, childish little snores ringing in the air, which has the turpentine smell of his glossy new Olympique Lyonnais posters. Then we go out to the living room where Tano switches on the television. Every channel, it seems, is filled with people arguing with each other about the upcoming presidential elections.

Paris may have earned its reputation throughout France—and the world—as being snobby, culturally speaking, but this attitude does not go hand in hand with any socioeconomic stereotypes; politically, the city leans strongly to the left. This is very different from Lyon, considered to be the most bourgeois city in all of France, not just because of its wealthy old families, but because it is a hub of the far right, *le Front National*, as well as the *Union pour un Mouvement Populaire*, referred to more simply as the UMP, parties that in political terms are equivalent to the Conservative/Republican parties in the United States.

Nicolas Sarkozy, of the UMP, became president of France in 2007, while we still lived in Paris. At the time he beat out the socialist candidate, Ségolène Royale, who was also the first French woman ever to run for president. Now, in 2012, Royale's former boyfriend and the father of her four children, François Hollande, is running against Sarkozy to be the new president of *la République Française*. And to the dismay of the wealthy Lyonnais of the Carré d'Or, it looks like he just might win.

Debate is the national sport in France, and Tano totally gets into it. "Don't you want to watch some of this?" he says, already riveted by the shouting emanating from the screen.

"In a minute," I say. "I'm trying to look for an office over here."

I have switched on the computer and am madly scrolling through pages, back on the office question. So much hoopla comes from the direction of the TV, and Tano seems so thoroughly humored, though, I cannot focus.

I join him on the sofa. "What on earth is so funny?"

"The French!" he hoots. "They are just so *abstract*."

This is the sort of analysis that rarely if ever will cause me to laugh out loud. All that arguing about theoretical abstractions is the stuff that I find supremely boring, and when played out in French, largely incomprehensible.

Besides, I don't need these tedious televised debates when I have the Charlie's Angels to coach me in the presidential race. While there may be a journalistic respect for the private lives of politicians in France, this *hush hush* attitude does not extend to the codes of gossip of the layperson, or at least not the layperson at place des Célestins.

While the rest of France blabs on about Hollande's social plan versus Sarkozy's mixed agenda, my ears are filled with analyses of the contenders' love lives. Hollande had cheated on and dumped Segolène for Valérie, who, if Hollande won, would become the first "First Girlfriend" as they were not yet married, and did not plan to be.

The main dissection that takes place on the steps of Célestins though, has to do with Carla's presence at the Elysée. The Elysée, of course, being the presidential palace and Carla being Carla Bruni, the wealthy Italian fashion model and singer who married Sarkozy shortly after he landed the presidency in 2007. At the time, he was married to Cécilia, also beautiful, in an icy sort of way, and who, when the marriage crumbled, promptly took off for New York where she married *her* boyfriend. After a very public courtship of Carla, which included a photo shoot at Disneyland that left much of France aghast, Sarkozy and Carla married.

There was so *much* to analyze about Carla: her public declarations against monogamy, her checkered past (girlfriend of Mick

Jagger, Eric Clapton, and some millionaire older guy whom she then traded in for his son), her fabulous wardrobe, and the "validity" of her latest album, in which she sang all about the orgiastic relationship she enjoyed with Sarkozy.

The Angels find this disturbing. I mean, *vraiment*: How could she sing songs like *that* about the president of la République Française? He who was already too *bling*, even for some of his supporters.

Not only do I find it amazing that the Charlie's Angels are so shocked by Carla's silly sexy ballads, but that it seems to add insult to injury of the bling of the Sarkozy presidency. In fact, the Sarkozy presidency and all of its bling looks to me exactly like this new corner of France that we now live in. *Très bling*, indeed.

The next day I ask Béné why she, who openly supports Sarkozy, cares so much about these details.

"*Parce que ça ne se fait pas.*"

Because that just *isn't* done.

Oh what a love/hate relationship I have with "ça ne se fait pas." If the American expression "it's all good," (even when it really is *not* all good), captures a certain pandering side to the American psyche, "ça ne se fait pas" captures all that is rigid and dogmatic about the French. And while every culture has rules, the French certainty that *subjective* matters have absolute rights and wrongs seems to sum up one of our main cultural differences.

Example: I ask the waiter in a popular *crêperie* to please cut the single gooey dessert crêpe we have ordered for the kids in half, and bring it to the table on two plates.

He refuses. "Ca ne se fait pas."

Nor can presidents and their fashionista wives be flashy.

It must be wonderful to be so certain of the order of things. Such conviction certainly provides a sense of security. Of place. Of purpose, even. For those of us who live between cultures, the first thing to go missing is any certainty, any absolutes, of the way things "really" are.

Twenty-Eight

Then my grandmother, my mother's mother, dies.

It is a Monday evening in Paris when I get the news, on my way from the office to dinner with a friend.

It shouldn't have come as a surprise. Gaga, as we called her, was 98 years old, after all, and had been in failing health for some time. But still, her death is a shock, and her loss jolts me also in that way of discovering how my destiny has been aligned with that of my parents.

With the news of Gaga's death, I become my father, the sibling who was always too far away to participate in important family events. The family dramas that played out stateside when we lived overseas—situations of alcoholism or illness or aging that required family interventions—were always matters that fell on my aunts' and uncles' shoulders. I know my father participated as much as he could long distance, by letter, for of course this was all before the age of e-mail, but for all intents and purposes, he was unavailable.

I know my father suffered over this. He never said anything directly, but I can recall more than once listening to the adults catch up over summer dinners at my grandparents' house in Massachusetts, my aunts explaining how and why decisions had been taken over the course of the past year. My father always raised his hands as though to say, "Don't worry, I won't protest any of your decisions." Often I heard him say, "I'm sorry I wasn't able to help you with that."

Now back in the States my family joins together to pay their final respects, and to be together in grief. My sisters report that my mother is beside herself at the loss of her mother. The rest of the family rallies around her.

I hate not being there.

I hate it because I want to be there with my family and I want to pay my last respects to Gaga, who was an amazing and strong woman, independent in a way that was radical for her time. And I also hate not being there because I was separated from my family for all the other nodal events that have taken place since my sisters and I became adults: the births of my own children, my sister's children, and the losses of both my paternal grandparents. (I was in Argentina for my brother-in-law's wedding when my grandfather died, and I was in Kenya starting my married life when my grandmother died.)

Some people might say, "Well, if you cared so much, why didn't you just go back for these important moments?"

The answer is simple: *Money.*

We just didn't have the money.

The ideal way to be an expat is to be cared for by a generous sponsoring agency (or to be independently wealthy), so that the periodic desire (or need) to return to one's passport country, with one's children and spouse, does not tally up to a bill of thousands.

Unfortunately, my adult life as an expat has never been cushioned with a lot of excess cash. Already most of our surplus income went to plane tickets to the United States or Argentina, as we were not in France as "expats," meaning, there was no sponsoring agency willing to foot the bill to send us home once or twice a year. (Some years I just had to flat out ask my parents if they could pay for me and the kids to come see them. Otherwise we wouldn't have made it at all.)

This is the divide between intimacy and geography. I am overwhelmed with this desire to call my parents and ask for their guidance: *How do you cope with being so far away when important family events occur?* But my own suffering is hardly what's important right now, and I know from the e-mail that they are all at the funeral home making arrangements as I stand here on rue de Rivoli in Paris, France.

I feel so cut off.

I duck into a café and take a table in a dark corner. The waiter takes my order and retreats quickly when he sees the tears spill. I call Lyon.

Carmen answers on the third ring. "Mom?"

"Gaga died, honey." There is no easing her into the news. It just slips out before I can stop it.

"Oh, no!" She wails. "Poor Gaga. Can we go, Mom? Can we go to America?"

"No, honey. I don't think so." Over my words I hear Tano in the background: *What happened? Is Mom alright?*

Carmen tells him and he takes the phone. "I am very sorry," he says. "Very sad."

Gaga and Tano had a special bond. She came to see me in New Orleans when she was eighty-five years old. It was shortly after Tano and I had met, and her visit coincided with a long weekend that happened to fall on Tano's 34th birthday. I had just started my social work practicum, and couldn't get out of work to pick her up at the airport, so Tano went in my place. When I got home a few hours later, I found them sharing a beer in the garden of our little house in uptown New Orleans, Tano playing his guitar and Gaga tapping her feet in time to the music.

That evening Gaga took us out for dinner and over dessert she slid a card across the table to Tano.

Happy Birthday, she'd written. *It was love at first sight.*

"I just can't believe it," I cry quietly into the phone. "I always thought there'd still be another chance, you know?"

"I do," he says softly.

Tano's father died when Carmen was eighteen months old. At the time we were living in Uganda, and Tano's brother, Fernando, called to tell us that "Papi," as everyone called him, had died suddenly that morning, at home, of a heart attack.

The message was delivered to my ears, not Tano's, because Tano was in Paris. He had gone for a meeting but had ended up in the hospital, a fact I had only learned that morning when his colleague called to tell me.

"*Ce n'est pas pour vous inquietez,*" Tano's colleague said. I wasn't to be worried, but my husband had been hospitalized in Paris for an emergency surgery on two gluteal abscesses. Although I knew enough to know that as a medical condition this was not life-threatening, it was, nonetheless, a surgery performed under general anesthesia, and he was far away from us. Alone.

I reached him by telephone in the recovery room to tell him that his father had died. I'll never forget the sound he made—as though I had punched him—at the news. When we pieced the time frames together, it seemed that the heart attack probably took place while Tano was in surgery.

Against doctor's orders, Tano checked out of the hospital and began the grueling journey back to central Argentina: Paris to Buenos Aires, fourteen hours' nonstop flight; Buenos Aires to San Francisco, province of Cordoba, eight hours by road. All of this on post-operative buttocks.

What Tano was feeling is hard to explain. I can best do so by recounting that he arrived too late for his father's funeral, and could not bring himself to visit the gravesite at that time, or for many years thereafter. By the time he arrived at his childhood home, he was also sick with a post-operative infection coursing through his blood.

Back in Uganda, I felt something close to despair. Was this what life was supposed to be like? Cut off from the people we most loved by thousands of miles? I thought of my own aging parents. Did they worry about growing old with one of their children so far away? If one of them fell ill, would I manage to get there in time?

I was confronted by this very question a few years later. When Carmen was four years old, and we were settled in Paris, my father experienced a series of medical events that turned from mundane to worrisome to life-threatening almost overnight. He went into heart failure and was rushed to the hospital in Washington, DC, where it was declared that he needed immediate open-heart surgery.

Back in Paris, I first knew something awful was happening when I got home one afternoon and saw the blinking light on the phone. There were multiple messages from my mother, who was swearing at the French-speaking robot on my answering machine, one of those irritating varieties that would not just let you leave a message without going through "options." *Press 1 for this, 2 for that*, and so on.

Not a French speaker, my mother unwittingly left a series of frustrated messages that sounded something like: *Kristin? Hello? HELLO? It's an emergency. Dad is in the hospital and Oh God dammit what does this stupid machine want me to do?* SLAM.

And then a few more similar messages and finally just: *You need to come. You need to come to Washington right now.*

It was out of the question to leave Carmen in Paris. I had no idea how long I'd be gone, and as Tano traveled non-stop with his job I couldn't consider leaving her behind. I got her out of pre-school and we left, with almost the same rapidity with which she and I had left Uganda two years earlier.

The flight from Paris to Washington is roughly eight hours, and from the time I heard those messages and the time we arrived at Dulles Airport, fourteen, maybe fifteen hours had lapsed. As the plane coasted to land, tears streamed down my face: I had no idea if my father was still alive.

He was, and for four weeks I got to be part of my family again, fully involved in taking shifts at the hospital to be near my dad, to help take care of my mom, who was distressed by this brush with widowhood and the uncertainty around my father's recovery.

It was a gift to be present in the midst of a messy, scary, poignant moment in our family life.

Now Gaga is gone. My family of origin and my extended family is gathered together in Washington to say good-bye to her.

My little family is in Lyon.

And I am in Paris, the place I consider home, by myself.

Twenty-Nine

A few days later, when I get to the steps of Célestins for our regular Thursday afternoon encounter, I find Dom and Fanny huddled around Béné, who is in tears.

"What happened?" I ask, relieved in some small way to have someone else's crisis available to take my mind off my own.

They answer in unison: Jean-Sylvestre has *une liaison*.

I know little about Jean-Sylvestre other than the fact that he is a successful art dealer and part of the heavily photographed Lyonnais social scene. I have never met him in person but have seen his picture, with Béné on his arm, in the local style magazine. He is handsome, in a very French way: slight, wiry, with sharply chiseled features and slick, over-groomed hair.

Nothing Béné ever let on to would have made me suspect *this*. From everything she has divulged, Jean-Sylvestre is the perfect doting—and rich—boyfriend. For months I have watched her arrive on the Célestins scene looking fantastic, rested, and fully relaxed. And why wouldn't she be? She has a twice-weekly *femme de ménage* keeping her apartment tidy while she shops, goes to matinees, works out with her personal trainer, not to mention the regular *protocoles* she and Jean-Sylvestre enact without fail, every other day.

"*C'est très dur*," she says in a tremulous voice, and then blows her nose into a butterfly printed tissue that she special orders from the novelty shop off of place des Jacobins. "*Et c'est compliqué.* It started after he found out about Paul."

"Paul?"

Silence falls. Around us schoolchildren run in rambunctious circles, their laughter casting a lively contrast to the somber mood of our group.

"Can I tell her?" Fanny asks.

Béné shrugs.

"*Paul a été le petit cinq-à-sept de Béné,*" Fanny says, her tone hushed.

The cinq-à-sept, the five to seven, the euphemistic two hours between work and arrival home when… affairs are conducted?

"I think I misunderstood," I say. "I thought you said that it was Jean-Sylvestre who was—"

Béné waves away my comment. "I *did*, now he *is*."

"Well who is he involved with?"

"Some *pute*… and anyway, I don't really care. Dr. Barnie says the real problem is with my father. He says that we have a relationship *beaucoup trop fusionnelle.*"

Bénédicte is also the victim of a relationship trop fusionnelle? And what on earth could be the causal relationship between Jean-Sylvestre's liaison and Béné's relationship with her father?

As though she has read my mind, Béné offers, "Dr. Barnie says that since no man can compare to *Papa*, I can't stay faithful to anyone. I am constantly looking for the one who will compare to my *Papa poule.*"

Papa poule, roughly translated, is a doting father, which I suppose means, in this case, that no man other than her father can ever spoil her enough. Which is hard to grasp when you consider how Jean-Sylvestre spoils her.

"I see," I nod, as though I get it. "What about Paul?" I ask. "Is it serious? How did you meet him?"

She narrows her almond eyes, and Fanny and Dom giggle.

"*Une soirée libertine.*"

My heart hammers in my chest. A soirée libertine is a swinger's sex party, the likes of which I know really *do* exist—I read all about them in Catherine Millet's memoir *The Sexual Life of Catherine M*. Having found Millet's descriptions of getting screwed up against a tree in the Bois de Boulogne by seven different fellow libertins, and sprawling out and exchanging every manner of body fluid with other middle-aged humans at various *Club Echangistes* so gross, though, it never occurred to me that "real" people that I know would actually attend such events.

There are roughly three hundred things I want to ask about soirées libertines, among them: How do you feel sitting there in your underwear—or naked, for that matter—with a bunch of strangers around you? When a man approaches you, is it considered rude to look at his penis? (I mean, given the circumstances, I don't know how you'd avoid it). How do you feel when you see your own partner having sex with someone else? Do you kiss the strangers you have sex with? What if the condom breaks?

Do you even use condoms????????

My mind flashes to the angst that a bunch of condoms managed to arouse in me and I think of how going to a club échangiste would certainly put me over the edge. I don't actually articulate any of these things, but apparently I don't manage to hide my expression, because Béné laughs. "You are surprised? We only go from time to time."

I'm not sure if "we" means her and Jean-Sylvestre, or includes the other two Angels, but she adds, "Jean-Sylvestre introduced me to Paul. They used to ski together, and found each other *par coïncidence* at le club the last time we went."

Some coincidence, I think, but what I say is, "He introduces you to this guy at a club échangiste, gets jealous, and now uses it as an excuse to cheat on you?"

"It's because I saw Paul outside of his presence. He could not tolerate that I have a *jardin secret*."

Well this is certainly fascinating. I have heard countless analyses about the French "secret garden" from the mouths of gobsmacked Anglos, who marvel at the ostensible French tolerance of infidelity. I had always chalked this up to being yet another Anglo fantasy about our Gallic counterparts: that they screw around left and right and turn a blind eye to each other's shenanigans. Then again, Catherine Millet came out with a follow-up memoir in which she revealed the jealousy she suffered when her husband actually got involved with someone else beyond a quick roll in the hay.

So *voilà*—here is a real live French person with a secret garden, although it did not start out as secret given that her boyfriend organized the whole damn thing. Wow. Maybe I should direct Jean-Sylvestre to Millet's *Jalousie* book.

I am shocked and titillated all at once, but only realize I am gaping when Béné says, *"Ca va?"*

Truthfully, what I am now thinking about is how this story encapsulates my own mounting certainty that I am really boring sexually. I can imagine Tano saying, "oh, please," kind of like he did about pubic waxing, but it's hard to discard what the Angels say: that what these soirées are really about is keeping things lively in a couple, avoiding that dreaded middle-age end of sexual adventure.

No matter how I stretch my brain, though, I cannot imagine Tano proposing that we go to a soirée libertine (although if he did, I cannot imagine being brave enough to accept), or that if for some strange reason we did end up naked in a crowd, that he would happily watch me screw someone else. (Although if we did land in that situation I am sure he would choose the grossest, most unappealing, smelly person available just to make sure I wouldn't ever want to do *that* again.)

But I am not ready to divulge my own more inhibited leanings and so turn the conversation back in the other direction. "I'm still not clear on how this relates to you being trop fusionnelle."

Béné puffs her lips out, as though the answer is completely obvious. Then she offers forth a practically identical version of what she has already explained: "I commit to no man, so no man commits to me. Voilà."

"And you agree with this theory?"

"I'm not the psy."

Her conflict—or at least the way it's presented—disturbs me. Maybe it's a mark of my Anglo Puritanism that I find the analysis tinged with something borderline incestuous, or maybe it's because I am a behaviorally oriented therapist that I find the conclusiveness a lame excuse for not taking responsibility. Mostly I just find it peculiar that in this day and age someone would sit there quoting their shrink, as though what he says goes, regardless of how she feels about it.

In any case, all this information has plunged me into a daze. A vision of these sumptuous women as three-, four-, and five-year-old *petites copines* playing at this very site almost forty years ago melds into a less pleasant image of them rolling around at some club échangiste with a hairy guy that, in my mind's eye, looks suspiciously like disgraced IMF chief Dominique Strauss-Kahn.

Yuck.

The four of us lapse into silence. Béné's son throws garbage in the fountain, and we all stare, as though looking right through him. I turn toward her just as a long tear slides down her cheek and lands in her lap. I can see where it leaves a little wet stain on her jeans. Spontaneously I take her hand and she looks at me with an expression of gratitude.

I want to tell her what I know: that surviving an affair is a sort of kinship. Once it has happened to you, you discover that there are only certain people with which you can speak a sibling-like shorthand of betrayal, bewilderment, and the miserable revelation that only two choices remain: either you split up for good, or you stay together and wait for enough time—slow, slow, time—to pass so that you no longer think about your husband's affair all the time, every second of every waking hour. You become the master multi-tasker: at work, reading the kids their bedtime stories, chatting with the cashier at the grocery store, all the while thinking, somewhere in the far recesses of the mind, *he cheated on me, he cheated on me.*

And even then, when you think you have fully recovered, something will happen that in a flash takes you right back.

I don't offer all of that, not yet at least. For now I just say, "I've been through this with Tano."

All three Angels look shocked. I am surprised. Is it really *that* unbelievable?

I spell out a rough sketch of all that history that I have managed to avoid divulging thus far: that our happy union had once been so strained by the weight of lifestyle discordance, cultural differences, and our own personal shortcomings, that it had finally collapsed in a heap of messy infidelity.

"*Dis donc,*" Fanny says, "I thought you had the perfect marriage."

"I don't think anyone has the perfect marriage," I say. I am still holding Béné's hand, and at this, she squeezes tightly. Then she straightens, pulls her hand from mine, shakes her hair, and sighs, "This is a setback. But we will recover."

"You won't break up?" I ask.

"*Mais non,*" she says. "He doesn't *love* her—it was just sex."

My ears ring at the sound of these old familiar words, and I realize all at once how maybe I never understood anything about Tano's affair. Maybe none of us, man or woman, can ever fully make sense of another person's betrayal. People in "monogamous" relationships stray for so many reasons—boredom, anger, neglect, temptation, fun… And because this list is hardly exhaustive is the exact reason that forgiveness has to be an option. Maybe that's why that leap of faith—that things *can* heal and be okay again—matters so dearly.

"So what will you do?" I ask.

"I will ask Dr. Barnie to prolong my arrêt."

Whether the Charlie's Angels work or not is none of my business, but as a foreigner, I can't help but note the intensely different cultural attitudes related to work. It seems that in France, in spite of all the polemic about soaring unemployment, work is treated with suspicion, a sense of burden. There is no trace of the "pull yourself up by the bootstraps and get back to work" attitude that courses through American culture.

"You know," I say, measuring my words tentatively, "Maybe it's the opposite. Maybe going back to work would help you recover from this crisis."

All three Angels stare at me like I am *très bizarre*.

"No really," I say. "Maybe you'd feel better if you had an activity that was mentally stimulating."

"*C'est un point de vue très américain,*" they say, with no irony whatsoever. A *very* American viewpoint.

And there it is, that same old identity question: Do I believe in the healing benefits of hard work because I, the individual person, almost always believe action to be superior to analysis, or because I am American and that's how Americans function, in terms of what we *do*?

In any event, the irritation on the Angels' faces points to the fatuousness of pursuing this conversation.

Subject dropped.

Thirty

The Fête des Lumières—Festival of Lights—is a Lyonnais tradition that gives thanks to Mary, mother of Jesus Christ, every year on December eighth. The origins of the festival date back to the mid-1600s when Lyon was ravaged by the plague. The *échevins*—a sort of noble magistrate—prayed for the town to be saved, promising that if it were, Mary would be honored.

Contemporary tradition has it that in early December a huge MERCI MARIE lights up Fourvière Hill, while habitants throughout the city place votive candles, called *luminons*, in their windows. This, along with the spectacular sound and light shows that the city organizes, makes the Fête des Lumières a hugely popular event, by some estimates one of the biggest festivals in the world, in the same ranks as Rio de Janeiro's Carnaval and New Orleans's Mardi Gras.

The Lyonnais are known for being very proud of their city, and the Charlie's Angels are no exception. They are extremely animated about the light shows scheduled for this year, and discuss their plans to perambulate the city with their kids on the first night of the event. Apparently it is the least crowded of the four-day weekend.

"I'd love to have you all over to kick off the evening," I say, jumping on a chance to expand our social time beyond the steps of Célestins, unsure, even, if they were including me in their plans.

"I could prepare something to eat, and then we could venture out together."

Was I unconsciously assuming they wouldn't accept my invitation? Because when they all agree to come I am suddenly stressed. Like, *mega* stressed. How did I ever get this idea that preparing *food* for a group of bourgeois Lyonnais women would be a good idea?

That evening I sit on the edge of Carmen's bed, notebook and pencil in hand. "Help me," I moan.

"Calm down, Mom. It will be fine, as long as you keep the courses clearly divided."

She is referring to something that Deanna's husband, Regis, once commented on: that at parties thrown by Anglos, the sweet and the salty often ended up on the same table, served at the same time, the cheese torn into as an appetizer and other such barbaric practices.

In contrast to a formal French meal, my spreads did tend to get rather undisciplined, with no hard and fast rules as to the order in which you had to eat things.

Now I am counting on my daughter's Frenchness to help me figure out what to serve. We sit in silence.

"Well," she finally says, "it's not like you're going to prepare a *steak tartare*, so we can rule *that* out."

The image of that popular French dish—a plate of raw hamburger with an uncooked egg yolk quivering on top of it—suddenly strikes me as hilarious. We cackle with laughter.

"Maybe," I say, wiping tears from my eyes, "I should prepare Asian food."

Carmen's eyes light up. "We can go to Guillotière?"

Less than half a mile away, right across the Pont de la Guillotière, in the neighborhood by the same name, is the Asian quarter. The kids and I have been wandering over every couple of weeks to pick up exotic vegetables, tofu, and all sorts of frozen delicacies shipped straight from Vietnam, Thailand, and Cambodia. With the fresh green, yellow, and red curries available, we have been learning to make some stunningly delicious dishes. Perfect!

The first day of the Fête, however, Fanny backs out of our plans.

"*Mais non*," Béné protests. We are at Célestins, as usual, watching the kids run around amidst technicians doing last-minutes tweaks on what promises to be a superb light installation.

"Docteur Barnie says I'm not ready for crowds," she says. "I get panicky."

"Don't tell him," Dom argues. "Just come. We'll stick by you. It will be fine."

"But it's not me who decides," Fanny says, clearly annoyed by the pressure.

I am struck, as always, by that odd French reverence for authority. I hear my own voice saying what Dr. Michel always told me. "*Mais tu as le droit de…*"

But she cuts me off mid-"heal." "Dr. Barnie will tell me when I am cured." Her expression is firm, as in case closed.

At the very last minute, Dom backs out as well, so only Béné comes for dinner, pulling her son Victor up the stairs. Truthfully, I am happy, for Béné is the one I really feel a sense of affinity with, however tenuous. We bonded over the discovery of Jean-Sylvestre's liaison, and she is by far the least judgmental of the

Angels when it comes to my image and fashion problems. This does not prevent me from wanting to impress her, though, and so I feel nervous, almost like I am on a first date, helping her out of her coat, serving her a glass of *Côte du Rhône* (figuring I couldn't go wrong with a wine of the region), and nervously checking my curry in the kitchen. Tano thinks I am neurotic, running around as though I am serving the queen, but I shush him and send him to her with a little tray of apéro—peanuts, almonds, and olives.

Lorenzo and Victor stand at the window, watching the light show on the street below. Lorenzo is a full head taller than Victor, and from behind they could be mistaken as brothers, now that Victor has shed his preppy look for some more rumpled and scuffed items. I note how he bumps his hip into my son, who bumps him right back, until they are shoving and giggling and having a grand old time of it.

"Knock it off, guys," I say, almost in spite of myself, for I am still so delighted every time I witness this type of carefree, child's play. There is nothing in that happy-go-lucky horsing around that says my kid is down in the dumps anymore, and I am so relieved that the worst of the transition crisis seems to have passed.

Béné and I join the boys at the window. This year rue du Président Edouard Herriot is lit up in butterflies, their colorful wings flickering far down the street toward Hôtel du Ville, until we cannot see any further.

"The crowd is already huge," Béné says. She sounds exasperated. "When I was young the fête was the pride of Lyon. Now it's almost a nuisance. All these tourists."

As someone who hates crowds, I cannot help but agree. The sight of hundreds of people milling around on the street below makes my stomach clench, enough that were it not party-pooperish, I'd probably just stay home and catch what I could from five flights up.

But the kids are excited and the show awaits, and so I turn back to the kitchen to get dinner on the table. The curry has turned out beautifully, the sauce thick and bubbling, the coconut milk and fresh coriander announcing their presence clearly over the aroma of citronelle, garlic, and galangal.

"*Bon appétit!*" I say, and we dig in.

My family of four adores a good spicy curry. Tano's tongue was trained for it, day in and day out, the year he spent as the doctor in a Laotian refugee camp in Northern Thailand.

I grew to love spicy curries the two years I lived in India with my parents and sisters.

Carmen and Lorenzo have never been anywhere in Asia, but we have taken them to so many varieties of Asian restaurant, and used so much spice in our own cooking, it is a taste they acquired young.

It hadn't occurred to me that our guests might not share the same enthusiasm.

In fact, it only dawns on me when I see Béné pushing her food around the plate and taking tentative bites: a little rice, a little broccoli.

Poor Victor looks downright miserable. His fork is laid face down on his plate, a single piece of tofu with the tiniest trace of a nibble next to it.

Oh, dear.

"Is the food too spicy?"

"*Non, non,*" Béné says. "*C'est bon.* But perhaps Victor will just wait for *le fromage.*" She turns to Victor. "*D'accord, cheri? Tu attends le fromage.*"

Oh sure, fine. Victor's going to wait for the cheese course.

Except I don't have any cheese in the house.

Under the pretense of refilling the water pitcher, I run to the kitchen and fling open the fridge. In it I find a chunk of camembert that has already started to dry around the edges, and some grated emmental that has turned green.

Carmen joins me in the kitchen. "Are you getting the cheese course ready?"

We clutch each other with laughter, the kind that the more you try to stifle, the more uncontainable it becomes. "Shhhh!" I gasp. "They'll hear us!" I show her the molding emmental. Tears roll down our faces.

Then Carmen points and says, "Look, Mom!"

The light from the stove is on behind us, projecting our shapes onto the deep pink wall. Our shadow portraits are almost indistinguishable and our hair, in a frisson of static electricity, has created an ethereal halo between our two heads.

It seems to me that in this moment, this funny, bonding moment, something magical has happened. We are mother-daughter imagoes, our melded form cast on a rose-colored wall. Seen that way, the defining details of our lives, in which we are culturally different line up in perfect overlay with those ways in which, culturally, we are the same. In this light, the duality is invisible.

Screw le fromage. And let that be a lesson in cultural diversity for my daughter: not everyone's world revolves around the cheese course.

"Sorry friends," I announce, carrying an assortment of yogurts and compotes out to the table. "There is no cheese."

No cheese? Béné and Victor are quite visibly shocked. Although it is also possible that I am just projecting my own deluded fantasy about the French and their fromage. For all I know they don't give a rat's ass if there is cheese. Maybe they just assumed there would be the way people assume that there will be turkey and mashed potatoes on Thanksgiving.

Victor nibbles at some applesauce while Béné continues to pick at her curry.

Later she helps me clear the plates and apologizes that Victor didn't eat more.

"It's my fault. I should have been aware that not everyone likes spice."

"Yes, I suppose you of all people," she giggles knowingly and nudges me in the ribs.

The words hang there—I truly don't get it—and then I do: We're back on blow jobs.

"No fair!" I attempt a guffaw, but only because I am embarrassed. And offended. Clearly Béné sees me as a big fat goody-two-shoes.

Like any defensive human being, my first instinct is to protest. I think of announcing how I did my fair share of sleeping around in college. Or that I was once the proud owner of a Rabbit Pearl, marketed as the "Rolls Royce" of vibrators. Or what about the crotchless underwear I shocked an unsuspecting ex boyfriend with?

But what am I trying to prove? There was a moment in time when I would have died to be considered the boring old prude. I remember vividly when Tano's affair was revealed how I imagined everyone in the know must have thought that I was less of a woman, less of a lover, inadequate: otherwise, why would he be cheating on me? Too fat, too thin, too flat chested, too booby, never just right, never good enough, and every step of the way evaluating the infidelity according to that terrible notion that it all came down to something being wrong with *me*. It took years for me to grasp that a man who claimed to love me could also cheat on me, and that in many ways, it had nothing to do with me at all, and everything to do with how he felt about himself in our relationship.

Suddenly Béné drops a glass, and it shatters around our feet, sharp splinters and shards flecked with red wine. It looks like blood. Béné is horrified, but I totally don't care. It's just a silly accident, and the wine glass has no value, but she cannot stop apologizing. I see her suddenly in a different light, no longer protected by her swanky, sexy image but human, fallible, capable of being a klutz and fearing that she will be judged. And just like that, watching this sophisticated woman bumble around, there is some slight shift back to what I *know*, and I think: who cares what Béné thinks of my sex life?

And so I don't tell her a damn thing about all the ways I was *not* a goody two shoes, all the ways in which I am just now, a woman in my early forties, finally making sense of what it means to be in a long-term relationship, warts and all.

Instead, I suggest that we round up the kids, and we head out into the Fête des Lumières. I'm just glad this isn't Carnaval in Rio because I swear to God I wouldn't be caught dead dancing down the road in a thong.

Thirty-One

For reasons that at the time seem like good ones, I declare that since I am not yet working in Lyon, now is the right time to get the kittens. Never mind that my exhaustion is real, and never mind that the housework is still the bane of my existence. I am as stretched as ever but believe that adding two animals to the mix will improve our lives.

I look up the SPA—*la Société Protectrice des Animaux*—the French equivalent of the Humane Society, and cannot believe my bad luck. There are only *six* kittens in the whole Rhône-Alpes region available for adoption! And from their photos on the website, they are all so adorable they will certainly be taken immediately by some other families. I would charge out and pick two while the kids are at school, but this is no easy feat given that the SPA is forty minutes away by car, a complicated journey for the car-less.

So I telephone, repeatedly, but no one ever answers, forcing me to leave long, detailed messages: Please please *please* reserve two of those six kittens for us. We are new in town, my son is just barely recovered from a major adaptation crisis, and an adorable kitten could seal the deal on our newfound tranquility.

I debate whether I should lie that I am handicapped.

The fifth time I call in a two-hour span, a brusque woman answers and cuts me off mid-speech. There is no reserving, she says. Just get out here, fast.

Saturday morning, after which Tano and I have enacted our protocol of having no sex all night long, I roll out of bed and charge, kids in tow, to the SPA. The cat-loving mother of one of Carmen's friends has offered to drive us, and in the car on the way over she fills our ears with animated chatter about the joy of pets—something my kids will experience for the first time ever.

Upon arrival it is immediately clear how completely insane my messages must have been to anyone at the SPA. Because there are hundreds of cats at the shelter. Hundreds of kittens. Apparently their website is updated about once every decade, so the six kittens we drooled over are long gone.

We go through cabin after cabin of cats—they are all so cute I don't know how we'll ever decide—but the kids fall instantly in love with a fuzzy female tortoise shell who must only be six weeks old, and a male ginger who is only just a month or so older. We name them Olive and Gaspard on the spot.

Getting the kittens infuses Lorenzo with something I can only describe as jubilation, and Carmen literally floats around with the ethereal aura of a first-time mother. That it all goes so well is fantastic, as less than twenty-four hours later I have to leave for Paris. Although Tano is a natural with animals, having grown up with dogs, cats, horses and cows, he has made it patently clear that we can get the pets, but that he is exempt from all caretaking duties.

So with the kids fully in charge of the kitten project, off I go on Sunday night to earn my living in Paris.

On Monday evening I get the report from Lyon: All is well.

But on Tuesday morning, as I step off the metro at Invalides, a terrifying message pops up on my phone:

Carmen: Mom, I think the kittens have diarrhea.

Me: You think or you know?

Carmen: Well, there's a puddle of something brown and runny in the hallway. And footprints.

Me: Footprints?

Carmen: Of the same brown stuff. Like they stepped in it.

I dial the house and Tano answers on the first ring.

"Get involved," I say.

"Not to worry," he answers.

I am both relieved and grateful, until he adds, "Until you get back."

Carmen begs (and is granted) permission to stay home from school to look after Olive and Gaspard, and I feel my tension flare with every diarrheal update that I am privy to between sessions (If people only knew what therapists are *really* thinking about when we nod our heads and say *mmm-hmmmm*.)

I race for the train to Lyon that evening and leap on just as the doors close. I am tired and hungry and not looking forward at all to dealing with cat poop issues. I reach my seat and discover that I am in a *quarto*—my least favorite arrangement, where four seats are in a cubicle around a table. There are three businessmen already in their places, and I slide into my seat, saying, "*Bonsoir.*"

Then I lean my head against the seat and take deep breaths. For a few minutes, the lull of the train pulls me into that delicious type of sleep that comes on heavy and unstoppable. The ear-piercing message from the conductor, about the snack bar in *voiture quatre* breaks into that comfort, and I blink open my eyes to the piercing gaze of the passenger seated before me. I look away, yawning, not even really registering his presence. But when I look back a moment later, he is still looking at me. He smiles and nods and I snap my eyes shut. A minute later I peek through my eyelashes. He's still staring! For the love of God, I wish he'd stop.

This is awkward. And I really don't feel like being the object of someone's erotic fascination at this moment. (Although part of me wishes the Charlie's Angels could see that some stranger apparently wants to enact un protocole with me, in spite of my ostensible invisibility.)

I take another little peek and allow my eyes to do a quick scan: He is balding, yet nice-looking, dressed in a good suit, necktie loosened. At another stage of my life I would likely have done some outrageous thing, like orchestrate a quickie in the bathroom. But at this point in time I can honestly say there would be few things more off-putting than some random penis swinging around in my face, poking me in the leg, growing clammy in my hand.

Ugh. I shudder. Then I drop my gaze to his shoe, easily visible because of his one leg crossed over his knee, sticking out into the aisle. The shoe is a brown suede lace-up, quite similar, really, to the kind Tano wears.

He fiddles with the shoelace and then I notice his wedding ring.

OH MY GOD.

His poor wife is probably slaving away with the housework and the kids somewhere and getting all of her pubic hair yanked off just to keep him happy while he's on this train trying to get some jardin secret going. What a jerk.

I squeeze my eyes shut and will him to change seats. But with my eyes closed and the gentle rocking of the train, even my annoyance cannot prevent the day's fatigue from catching up to me, and my mind softens around the edges. I am rapidly back in that middle place between sleep and wakefulness, where I am still conscious, somehow, of light and sound outside me, but inside, I am burrowing further and deeper to some soft core where memory is stored.

I land on an image of my father arriving home from the US Embassy one night when we lived in Cairo. While he was at work we adopted a puppy, and while this in itself was news, the REALLY big news about it was that we did this even though he had declared a ban—for life—on pets, when the dog he had adopted for us years earlier, when we still lived in DC, peed all over the house, destroying the brand new wall-to-wall carpeting.

"Where did that animal come from?" he gaped.

"Upstairs," my mother answered. "From the Bensimons."

The Bensimons were our Israeli neighbors on the second floor. Their dog had just given birth, and it was my mother's idea to go up and "just see" the puppies. Of course it took all of five seconds before we were all desperately in love with the fuzzy babies, but it was undeniably my mother's idea to take one home with us.

She proudly announced this fact to my father—*I wanted her!*—as we all stood there looking at the puppy, whom we had already named Misty. We were entirely unprepared, though, when Misty jumped up on the bed and pooped on my father's pillow.

"That's it!" he bellowed. "The dog goes!"

To add insult to injury, the four of us female members of the house were doubled over in hysterical giggles. And then we begged and pleaded, and my Dad was outnumbered, so he finally agreed that we could keep her—on one condition: When we moved, whenever that would be, the dog would stay.

Of course we agreed. The impulse of instant gratification and our newfound love for this adorable creature blinded us to the emotional consequences of a temporary adoption. Deep down I suppose we thought Dad would eventually change his mind. And besides, when would we really be moving? We had gone to the Ivory Coast on a two-year assignment and ended up staying for four. Now we were six months into a two-year post in Cairo, but who was to say what that would really translate into?

But Cairo *was* a two-year assignment. We received news that we were moving to New Delhi six months before we actually needed to be there. "You have half a year to find the dog a home," my father said.

It was heartbreak, handing our beloved Misty over to the family that would take care of her for the rest of her days (they were also Foreign Service and lucky dog Misty ended up posted to Rome before retiring to Washington).

How could Dad have done that to us? I sometimes wondered, especially during that period of young adulthood when I felt that everything wrong in my life was my parents' fault. At a certain moment that question would share think-time with: How could my mother have done that to *him?*

To this day I do not know what had transpired between her and my father in the days leading up to the moment when she decided, unilaterally, that we'd adopt a puppy, regardless of how much he professed to hate household animals. Suddenly I can't help but think that maybe getting Misty was not some impulsive whimsy. Maybe it was a deliberate act of resistance; some way to take back whatever control she felt she'd lost.

Had I done some variation on the same by getting kittens that Tano didn't really want?

Suddenly my phone buzzes in my pocket, and those old images click from my mind as though someone has just disconnected the power. It is another text message from Carmen:

When are you coming, Mom? The situation with Olive and Gaspard is getting serious.

I catch Don Juan still staring at me. For God's sake. Could he give it a rest? Does it not occur to him that a woman might have more important matters on her mind? I shoot him the look of death. Surprise surprise: he looks away.

It occurs to me that the very thing the Angels have warned me about—sexual invisibility—is actually a gift. How liberating it is to *not* be under observation; to just mind your own damn business and be self-contained, especially when there's a diarrhea crisis underway.

The phone buzzes again in my pocket.

Shit.

No pun intended.

Thirty-Two

The next day our Wednesday routine is broken up by an emergency trip to the vet, whose office is on the other side of place Bellecour, just a few minutes from our apartment.

I get the stinky fur balls into their carrier and Lorenzo and I charge across the plaza, the cats mewling all the way. The vet's waiting room is full of pets and their owners, all of whom have the same high styling look of Lorenzo's school crowd: showy clothes, fancy shoes, even the animals wear diamond studded collars.

But the vet himself looks like a farmer, in overalls and plaid, and his young, round face is friendly. He handles the kittens (who, by some act of grace, have not pooped on each other) with incredible ease—they seem to mold to his big hands and ply into whatever position he needs. He interviews me in great detail about their lives thus far. Then he prescribes antibiotics for their diarrhea, and for their anxiety, cat valium.

Cat valium?

"*Mais oui,*" he says, in a tone that is oddly reminiscent of the dreamy Dr. Michel. "Can't you see that they are very nervous? Especially the male. He is dominated by this female, who is half his age. He needs something to help him relax."

Well! I'm not sure what is more stunning: the analysis of the gender dynamics of our kittens or that there is actually a drug they are going to take. I only half listen as the vet explains the treatment, as the rest of my mind is occupied with what I am sure will be Tano's reaction: *You spent thirty euros on CAT VALIUM?*

I fork over my credit card.

At home, Lorenzo and I give the kitties their antibiotic and then I try to get the valium down their throats. But pushy Olive shoves her way in and snarfs it all down before Gaspard has even tasted it, and then I really do think, "Get some balls, Gaspy." But he skulks away, and I resolve that when he is due for his next dose, I will close the door to keep Olive the dominatrix out.

That evening I am preparing dinner when I hear Carmen say, "Oh no!"

Then Lorenzo, in as much of a whisper as he is capable: "Mom is going to be so mad."

Their voices come from my bedroom and I go down the hallway, expecting at any minute to put my foot in a puddle of poopy glop. But when I get to the door I see from their expressions that something far worse has happened.

"What is it?"

They point to my bed. At first I can't make sense of what I am looking for. Then I see it: A big wet stain, right in the middle of my beautiful new bedspread.

"It was Gaspard," they say. "We were just sitting here and all of a sudden he jumped up on your bed and peed."

We stare together for a moment, and then the smell hits my nostrils. I inhale deeply, tears welling. Irrational as it may sound, I feel betrayed. There I was getting him his stupid cat valium and trying to help him relax, and this is how he thanks me?

I strip my entire bed—the sharp, stinky urine has spread clean through the sheets—and shove as much as will fit into our tiny, European-style washing machine.

Then I call Deanna, who is back on her feet, in great spirits post-chemo, and as an expert on all things feline, delighted to advise me.

"Even if you wash the bedding repeatedly," she says, "cat pee has an enzyme that is very difficult to remove. To our human noses, washed fabric will smell clean, but the cats will still be able to smell their mark and will think they're supposed to do it there again."

Fucking shit.

"But, cats hate tinfoil," Deanna says. "So put tinfoil on the bed. Then they'll stay off of it."

For the rest of the evening we keep the cats out of my bedroom, but the next day, before I leave for the grocery store, I stretch several sheets of aluminum foil across the bed. When I get home a few hours later, Olive is sprawled out—on the tinfoil—in the middle of my bed.

I call Deanna. "Olive does *not* hate tinfoil."

"Try pepper. That usually works."

Over the next few days I take to sprinkling pepper all over our bed, once in the morning, once at night. Tano thinks we have allergies we are sneezing so much, and I don't bother correcting him. At least the cats keep away from our bed now, and I am desperate to get the peeing issue under control before I go back to Paris.

Back in Paris I conduct furtive phone conversations with Carmen. "Did you sprinkle the pepper?"

"Affirmative."

But when the cat's away… or in this case, when the hysterical human is away, the cats *will* pee outside their litter box again, because when I get back from Paris I can smell it right away.

"Oh no," I moan, sniffing around our bedroom, not bothering anymore to hide this drama from Tano. "I can smell it but I can't figure out *where* they peed this time."

"This is very bad," he says as he undresses for his shower. "Pee, and last night I found something like dirt all over my pillow."

"Dirt?"

"Yes. Something gritty. Almost like pepper."

"Strange," I say, making a mental note to remind Carmen not to sprinkle it so close to where we put our heads.

I plunge my hands into the clean laundry basket, thinking that I can start tackling the pile up of chores. But as I pull through the tangled heaps, the sharp odor hits my nostrils just as I register the damp sensation on my fingers.

"*OH NOOOOOO!*"

Lorenzo, who is already in bed, comes running from his room. "What's the matter?"

But I am on too much of a rampage to answer, dumping laundry on the floor and keening, "I'm gonna kill them!"

"Who?" he cries. "*Who?*"

"The cats!" I shriek, and he jumps, startled. "They peed in the CLEAN LAUNDRY!"

Lorenzo bursts into tears. "Why do you scream about cats to scare kids, Mom?"

Some combination of his anguish and poor grammar bring me straight back to reality and in that instant, I see myself as my son must see me: wild-eyed, crazed, *mean*. Why *do* I scream about cats to scare kids? What makes me so hysterical, so short-tempered that some pee (in the—*sob*—clean laundry) can reduce me to this?

My father's face flashes into my mind. Maybe this is some version of what it was like for him all those years, moving a wife and three daughters across continents. Talk about feeling out of control. Jesus. It always seemed so effortless, but I am just now realizing, that is because I had been a clueless, unobservant child. Though developmentally, that might have been on schedule, what I clearly had not understood was that both my parents must have suffered a great deal of stress every time we moved.

And to think how we had all laughed when Misty pooped on Dad's pillow. My God.

I call Deanna first thing in the morning and tell her how guilty I feel for my outburst.

"You're just exhausted," she says.

"Don't forget overwhelmed and pessimistic," I add. "How are you?"

"Oh, I'm fine," she says. "I just have cancer."

Indeed.

Lest I sound completely jaded at this point, I do realize that compared to what some people go through, it is a luxury that currently my biggest problems have to do with having a life divided between two fabulous French cities and two adorable kittens who are marking their territory in all the wrong places.

I need to take a serious chill pill.

I start a load of pee-soaked laundry and then lie down next to Lorenzo. He is still snoozing away—getting scared by someone who screams about cats is a sapping experience—and I rub his back to wake him. "Let's skip skateboarding," I say. "Carmen is having lunch with friends and going straight to guitar from there, so you and I could have a special day just for us."

It is a beautiful morning in late winter. We wander, hand in hand, across place Bellecour and over the bridge to the Quartier Saint-Jean, where we eat good-looking sandwiches at the quaint tables in an old boulangerie.

Lorenzo seems so happy in this moment that I am almost able to forget that I was a shrieking nightmare mother just ten hours earlier. Still, as we run for the funicular that will take us up Fourvière Hill—we have decided to hang out at the Roman ruins—the acid taste of last night's outburst rises up in my mouth.

My mood is clearly all out of whack, but I have been so busy fretting about Lorenzo and Paris and getting an office and the cats and the five flights that I have not been honest with myself about how my own precarious humor may affect my family. *Why do you scream about cats to scare kids, Mom?*

Guilt. Guilt. Guilt.

We get to the "old" amphitheater—once the site of gladiator battles and enough other such bloody scenes as to make my own contemporary psychodramas seem utterly ridiculous—and I lean back against the stones while Lorenzo jumps and climbs. I take deep breaths, and with each exhale remind myself of all I have to be grateful for.

I wish, dear Reader, that I could say that this is where the story takes a turn: that I realize that I am going nuts and that I quit my job in Paris right then and there to potty train my cats and be there full time for my family. That I realize right then and there that sometimes you *have* to take a leap of faith, and that the very independence I am defending is in itself a type of dependency: dependency on a life that I have clearly outgrown.

But that comes later.

What really happens next is that my phone rings and when I answer, what I hear on the other end of the line is so incomprehensibly *not* what I expect that I ask the woman to repeat herself.

Her statement goes something like this:

It has come to our attention that you do not have a French diploma and that you have been working as a therapist in France for the last ten years. According to the 2010 Law of BlahBlah, you should have been paying value-added-tax for the last two years. You owe la République Française 18,000 Euros.

Thirty-Three

At first I think there has been some terrible mistake.

I have always done everything by the book, paid tax bills on time and even declared every last cent of my income, contrary to the advice of many a French friend who said to hide as much of my earnings as I can. I think back to all the comments I blew off over the years: *Don't work too much. Ask to be paid in cash. Don't ever declare your full income.*

I had always chalked this up to cultural disparity between French and American attitudes about work. But abruptly I understand that this advice comes from a deeper understanding of how the system here sets you up to fail, if you are a small business, and if you play by the rules.

My second thought is that *I* am some terrible mistake—an idiot, really, who has deceived herself all these years into believing that I actually have a successful life for myself in France.

I feel totally, terrifyingly destabilized: a woman who has lost her financial independence in her marriage, and a foreigner who has just learned that her way of earning a living in her host country is deeply, fatally flawed.

While some grasp of this notion sinks into my big fat head, Lorenzo falls while he is charging down the steps of the amphitheater. Blood streams down his knees and his tortured wails rival those of the people who were put to death at this very spot thousands of years ago. Truthfully, I am on the verge of my own howling fit, but Lorenzo's immediate needs for comfort and care force me to keep my shit together.

When Tano gets home that evening, Lorenzo is patched up and good as new, watching a skateboarding DVD, while Carmen does her homework. The scene is nothing short of idyllic except for the fact that I am immobile on the couch in a state of despair.

How am I going to tell my husband that I am a total moron? Even though I know Tano will see me through this crisis, I can already imagine the look on his face when I tell him that I completely fucked up my taxes. Someone as organized as he is does not make mistakes like this. *Ever.*

I finally choke out my story as he looks at me in disbelief. Amazingly, neither child interrupts us, so there is nothing to hide behind. There is only the whole awful tale.

"Show me your accounts," he says and reluctantly I produce a few messy file folders with papers shoved in willy-nilly, spilling out at odd angles. "Well," he says, his tone admonishing. "Here's the first part of your problem."

"Can you help me get organized?" I whimper.

He looks like a soldier summoned to the battlefield. But while I hover around him, coaxing him on with cups of tea and plates of cookies, he spends the rest of the evening, into the wee hours, trying to put order to my mess, sighing when he finds documents with coffee stains, Lorenzo's sticky handprints, Carmen's doodles…

"Really, Querida. You should be embarrassed about this."

Not to worry, I think, for I am drowning in shame.

Then it's the next day and I'm in the office of Monsieur Fisc, some punctilious *expert comptable* I have found in the phone book. The term means "accountant," but translated literally, it means "expert counter." For the fee he is charging, I certainly hope he's an expert at counting.

I am sure stiff Monsieur Fisc has never dealt with someone like me before. My papers may now be beautifully ordered in one neat packet, thanks to Tano, but all other attempts to come off as a normal human being by proper French standards are relinquished at the door. I am a disheveled mess, weeping and asking for tissues, which apparently accounting offices do not keep on hand. Mr. Fisc finally buzzes his secretary to bring me a roll of toilet paper.

He looks over my previous year's tax returns and announces that indeed, according to some law that was made effective in 2010, any paramedical professional without a *French* diploma, and that includes psychotherapists, needed to charge their client's 20 percent value added tax (VAT)—and hand every last dime collected over to the government.

Je ne comprends pas is a petrifying understatement.

Monsieur Fisc hands me a legal pad and instructs me to draw the X and Y axes on an L shaped graph. He wants to show me how the 18,000-euro figure that I owe in back taxes was calculated based on my earnings—*before* deductions, which strikes me as particularly unfair—for the last two years. But when he realizes I have mixed up the X and Y axes, he proposes that we just skip the tutorial. He will do all the calculations and it will cost me a fortune, but maybe he can get the 18,000 euros down.

I shed fresh tears, yearning for something similar to what I always felt with Dr. Michel, some kind reassurance, and I wait for my expert counter to tell me that I have the "droit de guérir"—the right to heal and be okay. But he ushers me from his office, a stern look on his face, and offers not a single word of consolation.

When Tano comes home that evening I am weeping, again, in the kitchen.

"*Kreestin,*" he says, folding me into his chest. "It's not such a big deal."

I cry even harder into his shirt. It's a much bigger deal than he realizes. For two years I have been working just to pay taxes, as the expert counter's fancy math has already shown that the bulk of my last two years' profit (which is not that much anyway, after all my expenses) will be paid right back into the system.

But as much as that—excuse my French—really fucking sucks, I am now actually crying because the whole depressing situation has shed light on the reality that it is time to let go. I am crying because the very thing that I believed assured my personal stability is falling apart around me, because—and this is what 18,000 euros of back taxes really means—it only makes sense to travel for work when you earn enough money to offset the costs and still turn a profit. I have been dragging my ass to Paris every week, and spending most of what I earn in those two days just on keeping myself afloat. Trains, hotels, meals, and other typical overheads. And now 18,000 euros of back taxes? I am, in one fell swoop, being wiped out. And then some.

I wail into Tano's neck. "Working has put me out of business."

"Well I didn't need this tax crisis to tell you that," he says. "I've known that all along."

"Then why didn't you say anything?"

He looks at me in wonder. "It's all I've been saying. But you don't listen."

I float through the rest of the evening in a cloud of self-loathing. Later, aware of my unabating despair, Tano attempts to console me by pulling me toward him in bed. He is tender, comforting. But any thought of protocols and keeping your man *très happy à la française* has been completely squelched by the weight sitting squarely on my chest, squeezing my insides like a fist. I have to go back to Paris on Sunday—although the decision to fold up my practice has been made, I can't do it overnight—but I really don't know how I will manage to get out of this bed ever again.

"Relax," Tano murmurs. "Try to sleep."

"I wish I could just stay in Lyon with you and the kids." The tears flow silently, from the corners of my eyes down the sides of my face, forming little pools in my ears. It was not even a year ago that I fell in love with Amandine Fontaine's apartment and then barreled down to Lyon with visions of some fancy existence dancing in my head, prepared to "become" someone new, only to be reminded, quickly, brutally, that you can change location but you cannot change who you *are*, fundamentally.

And what I am is a foreigner in France. Always have been, always will be. I have a foreign husband. Foreign degrees. I may speak French, but I do so with serious flaws, not least of which is my inability to understand the legalese that any small business-person should have a grasp of.

I am suddenly furious at France, for being so... so... *French.*

Then I'm furious at Tano, for making me leave Paris, where everything in my life *worked.*

But that old fallback position of blaming my husband is passé, and I know it. The reality is that my current woes would have caught up with me in Paris as well as Lyon. The problem isn't location. It's me. My lack of business savvy. My disorganization. (Try as I might I cannot suppress the image of Tano waving a stack of mail at me and saying, "Are you ever going to open these? They've been sitting in this pile for weeks.")

I drift off in a harrowed sleep.

Thirty-Four

A few days later I sit bundled in a warm sweat suit, leaning over my laptop, taking notes off the *Pages Jaunes*—the yellow pages. I am going to find an office in Lyon, even if it just about kills me every time I have to cold call another unknown therapist to ask if they might, by any chance, happen to be subletting? As is the case in France, I have to introduce myself each time as "Madame" Duncombe, and no one is very receptive, and I feel totally ridiculous.

I am just about to dial another number when the phone rings in my hand. It's Pandora. I ignore it, but when she calls back a few seconds later I think maybe she has hurt herself, maybe she needs help.

"Pandora?" I say, clicking the "talk" button.

"*Ma chère*," she rasps, "Can you help me get my shopping up the stairs?"

I hate to sound uncharitable, but this is not the first time she has called me from the courtyard to be her personal Sherpa, and today I really resent the interruption, especially from someone who has taken to "advising" me on everything I am doing wrong on top of being "beaucoup trop fusionnée" with my kids. I buy the wrong wine. The wrong cheese. Fruit and veg from the wrong vendor.

I consider lying and saying I am not at home—she is calling me on my mobile, after all—but for all I know she can tap into my vibe and know exactly where I am. So I trudge down the stairs, *bise* her hello, and swing the enormous basket of fruit and flowers onto my shoulder.

We chat in slow, modulated puffs up the stairs. It is non-confrontational until she asks when I am headed back to Paris.

"On Sunday," I say. "Same as always."

"It is not good for you!" she lectures. "All this movement. All this stress. It will give you cancer."

My breath hitches.

"Bone cancer," she says, gripping her shoulder and wincing in pain. "Do you know?"

I feel disease creeping into the space between us and it chills me right down to my toes.

"I sense that you know disease…" She takes a phlegmy breath. "You, or someone you know…"

"I'm sorry, Pandora," I say, my voice shaking. "But I'm in a hurry." If she really is such a clairvoyant know-it-all she must be aware that I *am* giving up my Paris life, and I really don't want to hear any vision she may have about me, or Deanna, or anyone else I love.

"You fear death…" she says.

Well who doesn't?

"…so you cling to your children."

That old argument! Anger surges up inside me. What is with all this crap about individuating from your kids when they are still so small? I just don't get it. I don't want to get it. I stare coldly and say, "It's called taking care of them."

I feel her offense in the way she peels back, and for a minute she just looks like an old, wilted woman. By the time I get back into my apartment, my stressy feelings are compounded when I check my e-mail and find another message—that is three this week!—from someone in Lyon looking for an English-speaking therapist. It's the last thing I want to do, but maybe I will be forced to transform my messy, underfurnished living room on the hoity-toity rue du Président Edouard Herriot into an office. I sprawl out on the bed feeling overwhelmed.

When my phone rings I let it go to voicemail—God forbid it's Pandora again—but when a few minutes later it rings *again*, I answer. What if it's the expert-counter calling with more bad news?

But it's not Monsieur Fisc, and it's not Pandora. It is a young female voice on the other end of the line informing me that she is an orthophoniste. My first thought is that something has happened to Lorenzo, but then it sinks in: She is saying that she has an office available for sublease on place Bellecour and when can I come see it?

Is right now too soon?! I practically scream.

Then I charge across the square, and five minutes later am shaking the hand of Géraldine, the speech therapist. Her lovely office is on the top floor of an aristocratic stone building on place Bellecour. It is an address that oozes prestige, yet it takes all of five seconds to realize that Géraldine is nothing like the other folk of the Carré d'Or, starting with the fact that she has wild unbrushed hair and a "fashion" sense as simple as my own.

She offers me a cup of tea, and I follow her into the kitchen to keep up with the non-stop string of information pouring from her mouth. She is also new to Lyon. She moved from Auvergne, the French countryside, to be with her boyfriend, Eric, a musician, but she really wonders if it was a mistake because he's on the road half the time and she's super lonely. Plus she rented this snazzy office from a recently retired psychologist (who I left a message for, which is how she got my number), but she had no idea how *prout prout* Bellecour was and she feels like a fish out of water but she doesn't have the money or the inclination to buy some fancy wardrobe…

She stops mid-sentence. "Forgive me," she says. "I've been talking your ear off. Tell me about you."

The details of my parallel existence tumble out in a flurry: Leaving Paris. Deanna's cancer. The five flights up. Lorenzo's adaptation crisis. Commuting. Trying to fit into the bourgeois bunch. My grandmother's death. Exhaustion. And then, on top of everything, the 18,000 euros.

Géraldine gasps at every worsening detail of my story, and says she is "*très, très desolée,*" and I know that she truly does understand, that her sympathetic words are not platitudes, as she is also in that fragile class of *travailleurs indépendents* who pay huge social charges and taxes and have none of the protections afforded the French salaried worker.

She tries to console me with an adage: *Les plaies financiers ne sont pas vitales.* Financial wounds are not life threatening. Then, without ever breaking eye contact, she reaches up the back of her shirt, and *one two three* off comes her bra. "I hope you don't mind," she says, "It was driving me crazy."

It's all I can do to not grab her and dance a little jig. *Enfin!* Someone down here I can relate to. And not just because she is casual and easy going, American style. Géraldine's life resembles mine in other ways that are uncanny, for she is also maintaining a life split in two. While I race back to Paris every Monday and Tuesday, Géraldine gets in the car and drives three hours into Auvergne every Friday afternoon. She recounts the same loss of confidence in her new life here in Lyon that I am going through. Géraldine also laments an absence of female friends to hang out with in Lyon, and I tell her about the Charlie's Angels. When I get to the part about the oeuf vibreur she roars with laughter.

"I can assure you," she says, "That is *not* a typical French secret."

"And l'épilation?" I ask, hopefully.

"Bah, oui," she says, "*Il faut.*" You must.

So crotch waxing is also the way to go in Auvergne. At least Géraldine does not gasp in horror to learn that she is in the company of someone who has a full tuft of pubic hair. *Au contraire,* she seems to agree that we are a match made in heaven, as she offers her hand and says I can set up shop in her office *tout de suite.*

We bise each other good-bye—*mwah! mwah!*—and I charge down to place Bellecour to call Tano.

I HAVE AN OFFICE IN LYON!

We get off the phone and I race to the furniture store up the street whose delivery people I tricked into believing I was handicapped. My new office is wonderful but it is not furnished with the therapy relationship in mind. Géraldine has a desk with one office chair behind it, and three hard plastic chairs for her patients. There are no comfortable chairs, no cushioned divan, no place to shlunk down for a conversation.

In the back of the store I find an armchair covered in black linen. It is on sale for 100 euros. Perfect! I sit down, lean my head back, and close my eyes.

Then I hear: *Madame!*

It is a snippy sales lady, done up in the style of the Carré d'Or. She probably thinks I'm a bum having a nap.

I snap to standing and say, "I'll take two of these chairs."

I recognize the look immediately: a mixture of bemusement and delight.

"*Vous avez un très joli accent, Madame. Vous venez d'où?*"

I am in such a good mood, I can't help myself: I tell her everything, from the shut down of my Paris practice to the latest detail about my new office. She seems genuinely sorry when she comes back from the stock room to say that there is not another chair like this one in stock, but that she can order it and it will be available in four weeks. No problem. I can just use Géraldine's desk chair in the meantime.

At home, I call all the people who have sought appointments in recent history. I feel like the little boy in *The Red Balloon*, as though I am trying to catch the life that has been bobbing ahead of me, dangling its string just out of my grasp. But within a matter of minutes I have four appointments set for the following week. I can hardly believe it.

That evening, Tano, Carmen, and Lorenzo accompany me back to the store to pick up the new chair. I boil over with excitement as we load it onto a caddy and weave down the street. The chair is not that heavy, and the building of my new office has an elevator anyway, so the entire process feels like child's play after the five flights hell we have been through.

While my family admires my new office and the view over place Bellecour, I place the chair just so in one angle of the room. Then I plunk down in it.

"Let's play therapy," I say. "I'll be the client. I want to see how it feels to sit in this chair."

So Tano wheels the office chair out from behind the desk and installs himself across from me. Only then do I see that my new armchair sits a good foot lower. If I use the desk chair, I will tower over my client, but if we change positions, I will sit much lower than the person I am working with. Either way, a bizarre body language dynamic is created.

"This is never going to work," I say, my mind flashing to the people I have booked to come in just six days from now. "I'll have to postpone starting sessions until the other armchair comes in."

"Wait a minute," Tano says, clearly alarmed by the idea that I might cancel my new work in Lyon before it's even begun. "What about *my* chair?" "His" chair is a black, faux leather recliner that he bought at IKEA, one of those distinctly masculine pieces of furniture that the kids love to spin each other around in and that he loves to sink back into to read the paper.

"Think about it," he says. "It's actually the perfect therapist's chair."

"You don't mind giving it up?"

"I'm not giving it up, Querida. We'll share."

And with that, my professional existence in Lyon is officially launched. For four weeks thereafter, anyone overlooking place Bellecour on a Thursday morning would see Tano carrying that leather recliner across the vast plaza on his head, and then, a day and a half later, on a Friday evening, crossing back with it, so that it can be used in our apartment until my office days.

Although getting that chair up and down the five flights is a major pain, I love these trips. We invariably end up in stitches, foolish as my handsome husband looks careening across the bourgeois place Bellecour with a big chair on his head.

The situation seems a contracted version of our divided lives: Paris to Lyon; Lyon to Paris; Herriot to Bellecour; Bellecour to Herriot. Back and forth, forth and back, always working, always organizing.

It occurs to me one night as we make the trip across Bellecour that this very scenario would fit beautifully into one of those talks I give to other expat spouses. It is the perfect metaphor for using what's available to craft a new reality. It also underlines how important it is to feel a sense of partnership with your spouse; that even if moving is hard and you sometimes think you hate him, the best thing you can do is enlist his help in creating the life you dream of.

"I honestly don't know what I would do without you," I say in the dim light of my office, as Tano puts the chair in place and wipes the sweat from his forehead.

We embrace at the window looking out over place Bellecour.

"Ditto, Querida," he says. "Ditto."

Thirty-Five

A few weeks later Monsieur Fisc gets back to me as I walk Lorenzo to school. There is no way around it: I owe back taxes for 2010 and 2011, and he can't find any loophole to knock it down a few thousand.

18,000 big buckaroos that I do not have.

I didn't think my mood could plummet any lower, but it does.

I blurt my update to the Angels at the school gate and they invite me to join them for coffee. Before the waiter has returned with our café crèmes, Béné says, "The best thing you could do right now is go on arrêt maladie."

"But I just subleased the office on Bellecour," I say. Then, thinking of what I learned during pregnancy, I add, "It won't work, anyway. Self-employed people don't get those benefits."

"Mental health is different," Dom insists. "You just have to meet with a psychiatrist from time to time and tell him how upset you are, and he'll give you a medical note to justify not working. The French government takes depression very seriously."

Well it can't hurt to ask, I think. Later, at home, I call the *caisse des professions libérales*—the department for self-employed laborers.

No such luck. In spite of the massive social charges I have paid over the years, there is no protection for me if *I* have to stop working. And right now all I want to do is stop, to forget this whole fiasco and bury my head in the sand.

But no can do, as I have my first client that evening. It is the wife of a professional athlete. She has just arrived in Lyon and is having a very hard adjustment: to France, to the French, and to the fact that she cannot work. "I don't know how I'll do this for three years!" she wails.

When we part ways she hugs me, tears still glistening in her eyes. "You must think I am crazy," she says, in her gorgeous Kiwi accent.

"You'd be surprised," I quip, hugging her back, and she laughs. Lord if she only knew.

Then I chat with Géraldine who is just wrapping up for the day. She has taken to referring to the tax officials as *les salopards*—bastard sons of bitches—and doesn't stop reminding me that financial wounds are not life-threatening.

"It's just such a drag," I sigh.

Then Géraldine, who I'm starting to realize speaks in adages, says, "*Aux grands maux les grands remèdes.*" In other words, desperate times call for desperate measures.

"What—you think I should commit suicide?"

"No. I think you need to beg."

"Beg?"

"Why not? The worst that can happen is les salopards ignore your pleas."

I stew around for the evening, but by morning I have decided that Géraldine is right. What can it hurt to supplicate the tax office with a proposition? I am a foreigner, after all, and an American one at that. They probably expect strange, inappropriate overtures from people like me.

Normally I would cajole Tano into writing this type of formal French business letter for me. Or in his absence, I would at least get Carmen to correct my spelling. But they are not here, and patience has never been my virtue, and so I do what I have never done in all these years here in France: I sit down at the computer and write a letter to the French Administration, all by myself.

Maybe it's because I have nothing left to lose that I actually manage to produce a letter that seems the perfect blend of stiff French formality and loosey-goosey Anglo-style "sharing." Even the grammar and spelling seem to flow easily.

I print it, sign it, and rush to the post office to send it registered mail.

When Tano and Carmen get home that evening, I tell them that I am feeling much better, that I have taken the bull by the horns. Would they like to see my letter? I shove it at them without waiting for the answer.

At first there are a few throat clears (Tano), then a giggle (Carmen).

"*What?*"

"Don't get so touchy," Tano says. "We can fix it before you send it."

"I already sent it."

"You sent *this* letter to the tax office?" Tano sounds like he's going to choke.

"Oh my God, Mom," Carmen adds. "Really?"

Thirty-Six

Dear Madame,
It was a very bad problem that struck me, caused by failure to under-
stand anything. It was because I did not know that I am a Value
Added Tax (this is beyond my comprehension). Meaning, I have not
make taxes for two years, or save enough to set the amount (for 2010
is 10,003 Euros and 2011 is 7,289 Euros).
I send you, dear Madame, this letter to seeking clemency for some
help. I pray to you, as I had no idea of this law change, and that's why
I have not managed correctly my situation. Now that I understand
I will do my best, with the assistance of the expert counter, to avoid
further problems. I ask for clemency because I was obliged to follow
my husband to Lyon (because he is a mutant) and since September,
2011 I had to reduce my ability to two days a week, with increase
in expenses. If I have to pay 18,000 VAT, I would not even afford to
continue.
Thank you for your assistance.
And please accept my most distinguished feelings,
Kristin Louise Duncombe

Thirty-Seven

"It was a very bad problem that struck you?" Tano howls. "And why did you call me a mutant?"

"You *pray* to the tax person, Mom?" Carmen adds. "You sound like a religious freak. Why didn't you wait for me to proofread it?"

That my child wonders why I didn't get her to proofread my business letter does not escape me. Who is taking care of whom here?

"I thought I had done a good job," I say, my eyes welling up, the tone of my voice begging for sympathy.

Of which none is offered, because Carmen has homework that she rightfully needs to focus on, and Tano is simply sick of my impulsive ways. I don't blame him. Instead, I sit down with the stack of unopened mail that he has again flapped at me. There are nine letters, eight of which are forwarded by our renters in Paris. Only one letter is actually local, and when I see that it is from the *Préfecture de Police* I literally think I am going to have a heart attack. Am I going to be arrested for tax evasion?

I swear to God, Monsieur, it wasn't on purpose!

But it is nothing more than a reminder that my *carte de séjour*, the document that allows me to live in France, is about to expire. Like, on Tuesday. And it is a much bigger headache to renew an expired card than one that is still valid. And so voilà, the decision to stay in Lyon next week, to not go through another chaotic trip to Paris, has just been made for me.

Thirty-Eight

Monday morning I get to the Préfecture at 7:00 a.m., as advised in the letter. It is a fifteen-minute walk from our apartment on rue du Président Edouard Herriot, and I tuck a cup of milky coffee in a thermal travel mug into my purse, next to the novel I plan to read in the waiting room.

That was the fantasy.

The reality is that already at this early hour, the line of people goes out the door and around the corner of the building. And it is presided over by armed officers! What do they think we're going to do: riot?

I look ahead at the 250 people who made it here before me this morning, mostly, it seems, African and eastern European immigrants. Many of them clutch dirty, photocopied documents that they fold and unfold as though it is currency (which in many ways, it is, as it is their only ticket into this country). From the looks of their shabby clothing and their difficulty communicating with the officers who holler things at random, the people I am in line with are clearly *far* worse off than I am.

Then one of the barking police officers approaches me to verify *my* reason for being in that line.

I prayed this wouldn't happen.

I would actually have given a kidney to not have to speak out loud.

But it is inevitable.

I state my *raison d'être*.

"*Mais vous avez un très joli accent, Madame. Vous venez d'où?*"

And so, amidst the throngs of the harassed underclass, many of whom live in shelters, or ten to a room in a relative's small apartment, the white, economically privileged American who rents an overpriced apartment on the most hoity-toity street of Lyon, gets *complimented*, for all to see, by the man with the badge and the gun.

I want to die.

And although I have not had any coffee that morning, and I already feel a caffeine-withdrawal headache starting behind my right eye, there is no way I am going to pull out my Starbucks travel mug and sip away like the spoiled person I am.

Nor do I whip it out when, two hours later, throbbing headache in process, I am finally seated before Clerk number 35, who wants to chat about his dream to travel the entire United States of America. I don't hear any other clerks telling their clients how they would kill to go to Burkina Faso, or Libya, or Syria. Nor do I hear anyone else being informed what I am informed: that my carte de séjour will not be renewed for another ten years.

No, this time it will be renewed for *life*.

Apparently, no one is suspicious of *me* (if they only knew I'm a white collar criminal), yet all around me other people are sent away, told to come back again tomorrow, or just flat-out denied any assurance that there is a place for them in France.

On my way out of the Préfecture, I give my coffee (and the fancy travel mug that has kept it hot over all these hours) to a beleaguered African woman with three small children.

Then I stumble down the street and push through the doors of the first café I come across, and go straight to the bar where I order two espressos from the barista behind the counter.

"*Mais vous avez un très joli*—"

I hold up one hand, as if to say, "hold on," while I use the other hand to gesticulate that something is wrong with my head. She looks at me strangely but serves the coffees.

I down them, one after the other, as fast as I can. Then I sit hunched over at the bar, waiting for the caffeine to kick in.

A horrible pressure pulses in my temples, but I pant through it, the way they tell you to when you give birth, one breath in, one breath out. I think of all those people I stood in line with at the Préfecture this morning. *Pant pant.* Then I think of all these sources of anguish that I have been reciting like the lines of a one-woman play: I've moved away from my home, *pant;* I live in a new city, *pant;* I don't have my own money and I can't start over, *pant pant pant.*

For years I saw myself as the victim of a frail union, and before that, a chronic traveler without a base. It's not all bad to have seen my life through that lens. While it was still relevant it gave me the strength to fight hard for what I needed: a home base and a solid relationship.

But it *matters* how you think about your story.

Matters how you tell it.

And I need to remember that now. Because I'm *not* a victim. I am one of the extremely lucky people in this world, and this surreal day, in which la République Française has just handed me a permanent residency card, has jolted the focus off of my sense of futility.

I may have some problems, yes, but my life is totally stable. My marriage is full of love, and my husband can and does support me financially. We have healthy, vibrant children, and no one is trying to boot me out of this beautiful country that provides us free education and medical care.

I have everything a person needs to thrive and I don't need to prove anything anymore. I might always have to fight against this deeply ingrained idea that I am a passive participant in a life that happens *to* me, where other people's prerogatives will always come first. That is the part of my life that has always led to feeling at odds with my so called "droit de guérir," for doesn't the belief that things will be okay have something to do with feeling like you have some power over what happens next?

And as I sit there in that lovely Lyonnais café, my headache lifting just the tiniest fraction as the caffeine hits it like chemo, a long-ago lesson that I seem lately to have forgotten occurs to me: In a context of plenty—security, shelter, food, education, medicine, and love—doesn't one *always* have power over what happens next? In a context of plenty, such as this one in which I live, doesn't my power comes from attitude; from being willing to take responsibility for the part that I can control, and to always at least try?

Thirty-Nine

In the end, in spite of—or maybe, *because* of—my failure to understand anything, the Tax Police cut me some slack.

Mais oui!

I am at my office on place Bellecour when I receive the phone call. So much time has lapsed since the original uproar that I have almost managed to put it out of my mind. Almost, but not entirely, for when the brisk woman on the other end of the line announces herself as one Madame Charpenne from the *Bureau des Impôts*, I immediately break into a cold sweat.

Me: I've been waiting for your call (nervous laugh). I thought you had forgotten…

Madame Charpenne: (all business) *Alors*, I am looking at the dossier that we received from Monsieur Fisc—

Me: Yes, he's my expert counter.

Madame Charpenne: And you owe back taxes for 2011. The precise sum is 7,300 euros.

Me: And how much do I owe for 2010?

Madame Charpenne:

Me: So, 7,300 euros for 2011 and for 2010…?

Madame Charpenne: (Loud coughing)

Me: I was just asking about 20—

Madame Charpenne: (More coughing) *Excusez-moi*. So, your total debt is 7,300 euros. Shall we set up a payment plan?"

The entire exchange is confusing, but I know enough not to insist. Later, when I recount the conversation to Géraldine, her interpretation is that les salopards have decided to grant me clemency for 2010, but they can't state it explicitly. Ignoring my question must be some sort of tacit agreement that I will only be held accountable for 2011.

At home that evening, I open a bottle of wine to celebrate. "I just can't believe it!" I say, spinning through the living room like a ballerina.

"They must have taken pity on you," Tano says.

"Or maybe they think you're mentally handicapped," Carmen adds. "And they don't want to make it even more difficult for you."

Whatever they think, I don't care to pursue it. I still half expect some deportation officer to show up at the door to rid la République Française of my lame ass.

But that doesn't happen, and the days tick by, and then it is really time to celebrate because Deanna has just received the "all clear" from her oncologist. There is no more evidence of cancer in her body, and though her breast is gone, and her hair has not entirely grown back, the message is that it's okay to dream again, to believe that actually, it's all gonna be okay.

A month later I lock up my Paris office for the very last time, and turn my keys back over to the landlord forever. Then I go by the Oberkampf kibbutz to see Susan and George, creeping into the building on tiptoes. I don't live here any longer, and I have finally accepted this. I want to come through quietly, like a ghost, checking in on my nearest and dearest but with no attention called to my presence.

We have time for a quick drink and Susan asks me if I want my file folder, the one hidden in the back of the highest shelf.

"No," I say. "If it's okay with you I'd like to just keep it stored away."

That weekend, Deanna trains down to Lyon to celebrate our new futures. Although this is not necessarily what her doctor meant by "You can relax," we figure that one night of debauchery can't hurt. I whip out the blender and the rum and mix up a big old pitcher of frozen strawberry daiquiris. By the time we finish it—and I am mixing up a second batch—we have Earth, Wind, and Fire blaring on the stereo—and we are all dancing, even the cats, curled in the kids' arms as they twirl and bump and grind.

The way Deanna is shakin' her booty, you would never imagine that she has just lost a breast and completed nine months of chemo. And the way I am doing the bump and singing at the top of my lungs, you would never imagine that I had been screaming about cats to scare kids, crying over finances, and basically feeling like a total wreck for the better part of a year.

Our celebration comes to a crashing halt when Pandora complains about the noise. We try to cajole her into joining us for a third round of daiquiris, but no such luck. Time to wrap it up.

In the wee hours of the morning, I wake to the sounds of the rabblerousers of place Bellecour. Something feels strange, yet it takes me a moment to realize what: *I feel peaceful.*

Tonight I don't jolt to consciousness, bathed in angst, remembering, in one mental flash flood, everything I am worried about. In spite of the noise, in spite of the late hour, in spite of everything that has transpired since I agreed to pack up my life in Paris, I feel totally secure.

I press myself closer into Tano's warmth. He lies on his side, swaddling me, our feet entangled, toasty warm after several hours under the covers. I sense, suddenly, that he is awake now, too, and I turn toward him, open to connection. As we move together my mind drifts to the minutiae of our happy domesticity, and that sense of profound closeness is more exciting than I might once have ever dreamed possible.

Afterwards, as we lay curled in each other's arms, it dawns on me what I am feeling: *At home.*

In that moment I know that never again will I think of myself as belonging, un-negotiably, to one geographic location. I had once thrilled to the idea of brick-and-mortar roots, and for ten years I had a life in Paris, on a kibbutz on rue Oberkampf. It was a beautiful chapter, and while it lasted, it gave me something I desperately needed: to say *here is where I belong and I can take care of myself.*

But I am no longer that woman.

Lying in this bed tonight in Lyon, France, is a woman who has stopped fighting childhood preconceptions of what it means to travel round the world on the wings of connection to another person. Lying in this bed is a woman who has learned to trust enough again to not have to be fully in control.

Tano and I may not have perfected any sexual protocols, and our middle-aged bodies might not win any awards, but oh, dear Reader, we have been loving each other for almost twenty years, across four continents, multiple moves, two beautiful children, innumerable joys, and some losses, too.

Home *was* in Paris, but it is in Lyon, now, too, because home will always be first and foremost in my loved ones.

"Tano?" I whisper. "Thank you."

"For what, Querida?"

"For encouraging me… to move, to make changes—"

"I always knew it would all turn out okay." He strokes my hair. "What was that thing that Dr. Whatshisname always said?"

"Dr. Michel?" I giggle.

"Yes."

"*Vous avez le droit de guérir,*" I whisper, and then, for good measure, I say it again. "*Vous avez le droit de guérir.*"

Those exalted words… They rang gloriously in the night.

You have the right to be okay.

And so I was.

And so we were.

Acknowledgements

If it takes a village to raise a child, it also takes one to create a story worth telling. Huge thanks to my beloved Paris family – Susan, George, and Matthew – of the Oberkampf kibbutz, and Deanna, my other non-DNA family member. You have all been such an important part of my life -*our* lives - I can honestly say I don't know what I would have done without you. Love you all.

Another huge dose of love and hugs to my DNA family: Mom, Dad, Lesley and Steph. Thank you for letting me write about you and about us, and for supporting me through thick and thin. I am one of the lucky ones who arrives at middle age with an intact and close-knit family of origin, and though I hate the geographic distance, at least we end up with a yearly reunion to look forward to!

I am grateful to have a fantastic group of friends, from many different chapters of life, and I appreciate all of the support you have given me over the years. Special mention to Kathleen Connors Bouchaud who has gone out of her way to support me as a writer. Cannot thank you enough for the multitude of ways you have encouraged me! Malini Morzaria, BFF forever...I will always be looking forward to our next reunion, from which I always leave with greater clarity about what to do next. Kimberly Komer Mousseron, MHC sister in France! Many thanks for all your support and the times in Montpellier that have been such fun. Aimee Pavitt, for filling that glaring lacuna of my new life in Lyon. Here's to friendship. Géraldine Tuffery, chapeau to you for being so damn awesome, and a grand merci for your big hearted support. Vive les filles de la Place Bellecour! To the wonderful women of the Paris Author's Group (and the token male French chef, Didier), thanks to all of you for being a fabulous sounding board. Special thanks to Samantha Vérant and Janina Rossiter for your help, interest, and friendship. Huge thanks, hugs, and long phone calls to my lovely pal, my fellow writer, and brilliant editor, also of the PAG and of the "let's drink wine and blab" club, Lizzie Harwood. To John Baxter, for all of your input over the years, thank you. You will always be my greatest editorial influence and I still cannot write something new without thinking of you and being on high alert for...boilerplate! To Claire Black: Thanks for reading an early draft of Five Flights Up. I look forward to the day I can return the favor. Jenna Land Free, editor, friend and voice of reason across the miles. Thank you for such solid guidance, and being a master tamer of my impulse control problems! My renewed love affair with Seattle started with you, and I cannot wait to share that bottle of wine! To Meg Bortin, editor, chef, and friend extraordinaire! I am grateful for the perseverance of our friendship over the years. There have been so many chapters – all interesting – I do believe we should write a book! Dominic Cappello, my dear, dear friend, my biggest cheerleader, my greatest mentor and partner in every sense of the word: thank you. We *are* family.

Last but definitely not least, endless thanks and all of my love to Tano, Carmen Makena, and Lorenzo. Without you, the story just wouldn't be the same.

The kids at place Bellecour, Lyon, summer 2011

Kristin Louise Duncombe is an American writer and psychotherapist who has lived in Europe since 2001. She has based her career on working with international and expatriate families following her own experience of growing up overseas as the child of a US diplomat and living internationally most of her adult life.

In addition to *Five Flights Up*, she is also the author of *Trailing: A Memoir*, a runner-up for 2013's Indie Book of the Year Award.

She currently resides in Geneva, Switzerland, with her Argentinean husband, two children, and two cats.

For more information, please visit her website:
www.kristinduncombe.com

13784033R00162

Printed in Poland
by Amazon Fulfillment
Poland Sp. z o.o., Wrocław